CW00546280

DESIRE
DISCRIMINATION
DETERMINATION

BLACK CHAMPIONS IN CYCLING

MARLON LEE MONCRIEFFE

Rapha.

Published in 2021 by Rapha Racing Ltd.
Imperial Works,
18 Tileyard,
London,
N7 9AH

Published for Rapha Editions, in arrangement with Bluetrain Publishing Ltd
bluetrainpublishing.com

Rapha founder and CEO: Simon Mottram
Publishing directors: Tom McMullen and Francois Convercey
Publishing co-ordinator: Melissa Richards

Editor: Guy Andrews
Publishing editor: Taz Darling
Art direction: Bluetrain
Copy-editor: Claire Read
Images: Linda Duong and Keith George

Book design: Leo Field
leofield.co.uk
Additional design: Cat Spivey
Typefaces: Martin by Vocal Type and Dapifer by Darden Studio

Printed in the UK by Pureprint Group

ISBN 978-1-912164-16-5

rapha.cc

For my father

An 18-year-old Cassius Clay out cycling in his hometown of Louisville, Kentucky 1960. Photograph by Steve Schapiro

I'M THE GREATEST
MUHAMMAD ALI

A bold claim. But the former world heavyweight boxing champion's success and self-belief originates from a significant moment in his life when he was a 12-year-old cyclist known as Cassius Clay. He rode to the annual Louisville Home Show on his pride and joy – a brand new Schwinn bicycle, in red. When he returned to where he'd left it, it was gone. Clay became so tearful and angry that on reporting the crime to a local police officer he promised to "whup" the thief if he ever found out who it was. The police officer suggested Clay might like to redirect his attention to boxing. It is still unknown who stole the bicycle, but every knockout punch he gave from then onwards was powered by the loss of his beloved red Schwinn – it became known as 'the red bike moment'.

It seems appropriate to start this book by invoking Ali, a man who throughout his life challenged the discriminatory colour line in the USA. He spoke loudly and directly to systemic racism, seeing it as greater than any opponent he faced in the boxing ring. It made him a champion of black people, of blackness, of black excellence. It made him an enduring champion of human rights.

But what of the activity he'd been taking part in on his way to that show in Louisville?

People are now talking more openly about racism and cycling. That's particularly been the case since the huge wave of Black Lives Matter anti-racism protests that followed the killing of the African American George Floyd, a black man trapped and suffocated to his death by a white American policeman in May 2020.

The cycling media suddenly started looking at racism to write their narrative of the black experience. For me – a black man, former racing cyclist, and an academic who had been researching and writing about the experience of black cycling champions for many years by that point – it was a peculiar thing to witness.

It reminded me of when I was at school and a white teacher asked me to leave the classroom after I spoke up about an issue from a black paradigm; a way of seeing and thinking different to dominant white norms, a perspective that they were not used to and did not want to understand. On my return to the classroom, I would discover white students being praised and given applause by the teacher for speaking a second-hand interpretation of the perspective that I had been offering. There is nothing stopping interested white writers from sharing their interpretations of the black experience in cycling. However, where this white narrative is given greater credibility than the black narrative voice and paradigm, this perpetuates racism.

I began developing my learning about the history of black cyclists and their participation in competitive cycling through my academic research project about black British cycling champions. I conceived this in 2009. Some of the key questions for me were: What are their stories? Why hadn't I seen them racing at the Olympics or at the world championships?

This book is the result of my original research project. I give my story as a racing cyclist and, as a researcher, I fuse my insights and experiences with those of a wide range of international cyclists from the past 120 years. I present and blend oral testimonies from their careers in cycling from grassroots level to aspirant to elite rider. What can we learn about cycling from the voices of these black cycling champions? What have been their experiences in the white-dominated world of cycling? What do they have to say about their sport?

Marlon Lee Moncrieffe

CHAPTER 1
BREAKING THE CHAIN

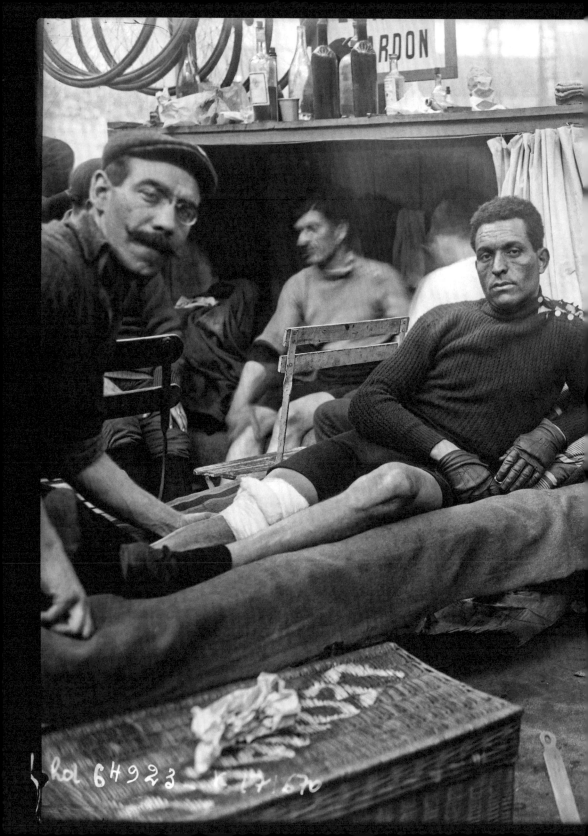

Ali Neffati was the first African to compete at the Tour de France. As a result the Tunisian became a popular rider at the European winter Six Day races. Here he's seen resting between races at the 1923 Paris Six Day race, held at the Velodrome d'Hiver

Over more than a century, thousands of riders have embarked on the unique challenge that is the Tour de France. They are increasingly drawn from all over the world, a pack with dozens of native tongues. Yet only a handful of Tour de France riders have been black. The first non-white rider arrived early: Ali Neffati rode in 1913 and 1914, a decade into the Tour's existence. But by 2011 Frenchman Yohann Gène was the race's sole black rider, a position occupied by Natnael Berhane in 2019 and Kévin Reza in 2020. In 107 editions of the race, the maximum number of black riders in the peloton has been two. We start this book with one of the better-known stories of a black competitor at the Tour de France; that of the Algerian Abdel-Kader Zaaf. Zaaf made it to the start line of the Tour on four occasions and also raced the Tour of Switzerland yet he is often mostly remembered for a bizarre incident on Stage 13 of the 1950 Tour from Perpignan to Nîmes.

SPORTING
EDITIONS SPÉCIALES PENDANT
LA GUERRE

Le départ de Paris - Tours

Early in the stage Zaaf broke away from the peloton with his compatriot Marcel Molines, the two of them building a lead over the pack of 30 minutes at one point. But the temperature was over 40°C that day and the heat began to take its toll on Zaaf. There was no team support and so, in desperation, he accepted bottles from spectators. After downing one such bottle, Zaaf lost control of his bicycle and started zigzagging across the road. With 40 kilometres of the stage still to go, he stepped off and took shade under a tree and went to sleep. His lead over the peloton was now diminishing rapidly. The roadside supporters woke him from his slumber, encouraging him with some urgency to remount his bicycle. Still in a state of confusion, he rode away in the direction he had come from and towards the approaching peloton. He was forced to dismount for a second time and was taken to hospital. Marcel Molines went on alone to win the stage. Zaaf left the race.

Speculation as to why Zaaf collapsed in such dramatic fashion was rife. Was it dehydration? Was it alcohol? Was it amphetamines? Was it all three combined? The media fanned the flames of debate and Zaaf's profile grew as a result, so much so that as the Tour continued without him he received invites to go and ride lucrative criterium races in Switzerland.

He returned to the Tour in 1951 and finished as Lanterne Rouge (last place), but his popularity and draw with the crowd was – despite his apparent cultural novelty – now the stuff of legend.

***

If top black male riders are rare, black female professional racing cyclists are rarer. Ask someone in the UK to name a black British female professional cyclist and the first name that would perhaps come to mind is that of BMX and track rider Shanaze Reade. Ask them to come up with a second and perhaps they would cite Paralympic cycling athlete Kadeena Cox. Ask them to name a third and they would be stumped.

Today, Dominican-born Dutch rider Ceylin del Carmen Alvarado has become the leading light, winning numerous cyclo-cross

World Cup events and European and world championship titles. When considering her Caribbean origin, it should be noted that Cuba has produced two female world champions on the track: Lisandra Guerra Rodriguez, who took two junior titles in 2005, and Yumari González, world elite scratch race champion in 2007 and 2009. The young Trinidadian road racer Teniel Campbell has become a frequent fixture in European races, and African American rider Ayesha McGowan has, late on in her career, found her way onto the WorldTour scene. France is carefully developing the promise of their 2019 junior world track sprint champion Marie-Divine Kouamé Taky and British Cycling is working with Imani Pereira-James – a London-born, Scottish socialised woman of Jamaican and Tanzanian ethnic heritage – for its junior academy programme. But, even so, there is no imminent prospect of significant numbers of black women taking their places among the pro ranks.

Why does cycling remain such a stubbornly white-dominated sport, particularly in representation at international level?

In some countries, the explanation lies at least in part in a history of legally enforced racial segregation. Jim Crow laws in the USA and the apartheid regime in South Africa both meant black cyclists were not permitted to race with white cyclists; not permitted to use the better cycling facilities such as white-owned cycling tracks.

This did not prevent black cyclists from forming their own groups or from running their own events, however. And there were some exceptional riders who by opportunity or initiative challenged the colour bar to break the chain of racism.

Take Kittie Knox. In 1893, this young black cyclist became a member of The League of American Wheelmen (LAW), a leading national membership organisation for cyclists in the United States of America. But a year later, to prevent what was seen by some as

African American infiltration of a white sport, LAW took the decision to enforce racial segregation laws and its racist committee challenged Kittie's membership. She stood firm.

Part of the Riverside Cycle Club – a black club based in in Boston, Massachusetts – Kittie was a talented racing cyclist with a powerful engine, as Joe Biel has written: "She placed in the top 20% of every ride that she ever competed in, many of which were at least 100 miles long. She was a faster and more skilled rider than most men. More importantly, Kittie made cycling appear fun rather than a complicated social activity."

She did not just challenge racism. Kittie also challenged perceptions of female cyclists, spearheading a burgeoning trend of wearing bloomers instead of traditional long dresses. Her innovative attire saw her secure victory in cycling dress parade competitions, experiencing the simultaneous endorsement and rejection of LAW judges as well as dismay and criticism from her white opponents in traditional dress.

When Kittie travelled to the LAW-organised annual cycling meeting at Asbury Park, New Jersey in July 1885 she was denied entry, as well as denied service by restaurants and hotels. Racial discrimination aimed to quell the desire of this brilliant young black woman. This could not stop her from forging her own path, being free to mix her cycling adventures with black and white people including

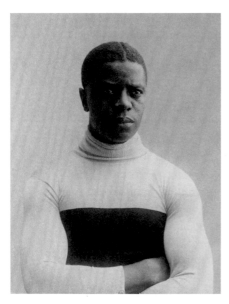

Left: Studio portrait of Major Taylor by the Paris-based photographer Jules Beau 1906
Right: Studio photograph from 1898, the year Taylor established seven world records

abroad in Paris, France in 1896. She died far too young, in 1900 at just 26 years old. What lives on is her defiance of the racist Jim Crow system which aimed to interfere with her love and freedom to cycle.

The impact of that system on the American black man as a professional cyclist is best understood through the career of Marshall 'Major' Taylor (1878-1932).

As a young boy, Marshall worked at a cycle shop. That he often wore military dress whilst performing tricks on his bicycle outside the shop led locals to nickname him 'Major'.

His eye-catching work at the shop also allowed him to meet and to become close friends with some of the best white cyclists in the world, including his mentors Louis 'Birdie' Munger and Arthur Zimmermann, the 1893 double world sprint champion. That social interaction forged an alliance that helped provide opportunities for him to race with white cyclists across the Jim Crow colour line.

One of Taylor's early victories against white cycling competition was in 1895 at the 75-mile road race from Indianapolis to Matthews, Indiana. The race was sponsored by cycling enthusiast and wealthy businessman George Catterson, who had become familiar with Taylor's cycling promise through conversations with Birdie Munger.

Fearing that white riders would withdraw their entries if they knew a black man would be lining up alongside them, Catterson decided to keep Taylor's presence at the race a secret. Taylor hid between trees as the race rolled out and then joined it from behind. He faced an angry reception from the white riders, including death threats if he did not leave the race. Rather than climb off his bike in acquiescence to the will of his opponents, Taylor pushed the pedals harder, ultimately breaking away from the pack. The day had begun with torrid and humid weather above, but as it progressed the clouds burst, and the rain poured heavily. The ground underneath Taylor's bike swelled to resemble the muddy conditions of winter cyclo-cross, so much so that this took its toll on the chasing pack. He was uncatchable and rode home solo and victorious.

VanNorman
PHOTO.
SPRINGFIELD. MAJOR TAYLOR

Despite his misfortune at the 1950 Tour de France, Abdel-Kader Zaaf became a household name in cycling. Here he is at the 1951 Tour signing autographs for the fans ahead of the third stage from Ghent to Le Tréport

Major Taylor racing with
Léon Hourlier at the Buffalo
Track in Paris, France 1909

It was an impressive win. But it was clear Taylor would always be
at the receiving end of racial slurs and threats to his life while riding
with white cyclists. For his own safety, he switched his plans to racing
and competing only with black people at shorter track distances such
as one-mile and half-mile sprints. He joined the See Saw Cycling Club
of Indianapolis, Indiana, and later, the Albion Cycling Team of
Worcester, Massachusetts.

In 1895 at the Black National Championship in Chicago, Taylor
faced Henry J Stewart – the 'St Louis Flyer', billed as the 'undisputed
king of black bike racing'. Taylor beat him, taking his first national
title and becoming the number one black champion cyclist of the USA.

But it was not enough for Major. He wanted to bring his talent and
powers to competition with white cyclists as well. And so, in defiance
of LAW, he began to show up at whites-only track race meetings.
When competition had ended, he would ride the track alone,
challenging the track speed records that had been set. His speed and
power meant he often bettered the records, much to the delight of the
crowds but to the disgust of the white racers. He was told his life

would be in danger if he ever again showed up to their meetings to embarrass them. Track owners who had sanctioned the record attempts were criticised by the white cyclists for allowing Taylor the opportunity.

Even so, news of his wins and various track records spread. He became acquainted with William Brady, a supremely influential Irish-American businessman and bicycle racing promoter. Brady applied his power and influence to LAW. From this, Taylor obtained a professional racing licence. His entry into the world of professional cycling began in 1896.

It would prove a mixed blessing. He became a wealthy man through hundreds of race victories, through his multiple track speed world records. He achieved two world championship victories in 1899; he officially became the USA's number one sprinter in 1900. He travelled across the world, racing, and beating the best, from national to newly crowned world sprint champions.

But all this glory and success was coupled with his having to endure abhorrent verbal and physical racist violence – from being face-planted into the track rails, to being strangled to near-death by a jealous white opponent.

When Taylor raced in Europe, he would often be referred to by the racially defamatory accolade of 'Nigger No.1'. 'Nigger No. 2' was attributed to Germain Ibron, a black cyclist from Martinique. He had been racing in France and across Europe, including in Great Britain, and like Taylor endured public emasculation of his ethnicity alongside praise for his cycling capabilities and potential. Taylor and Ibron were indeed champions. They broke the chain of racial segregation, and often took victory against the best of their white peers. But to retain a sense of human dignity that was being tested daily, they had to raise themselves above the challenges thrown at them, more so than their white peers in so many ways, not just on the bike.

The challenges faced by black people in the USA were mirrored in South Africa, mired as it was in the system of apartheid enforced by the white-ruled National Party from 1948 to the early 1990s.

Yet the country's gold mines proved fertile ground for bike racing, with black-only events running from the late 1950s to the mid-1980s. These events became so popular that the reverse of what had happened in the USA occurred: white cyclists began to break their own laws in their desire to take part in races with the black cyclists; to pit themselves against champions like John Moding, Pefeni Mtembu,

Siphiwe Ngwena, Jack Ntseou, Elias Ramantele and 'Skelm' Selatwe.

As time went on, South Africa's racist apartheid regime faced increasing criticism from around the world. Sanctions were imposed against the country. South Africa was excluded from the 1964 Olympic Games, and in 1970 the South African Cycling Federation (SACF) was suspended by the Union Cycliste Internationale (UCI), the sport's governing body. This meant South African cyclists were prevented from participating in any UCI races. The SACF was therefore forced to break its own chain of apartheid and to engage with black cyclists.

The country's first integrated competitive race was the 1973 Rapport Toer, an international cycling event held around Cape Town. Influential in its organisation was the white South African Basil Cohen.

The inaugural edition included three foreign squads made up of riders who had rebelled against their own government's ban on taking part in sporting events in South Africa. Most teams in this event, however, were white South African. The one black team, named 'Clover' after its sponsor, consisted of the mine workers: John Moding, Richard Moteka, Abie Oromeng and Elias Ramatele. It was Moding who shone the brightest amongst them in the race. He shared victory in the overall King of the Mountains points classification with the white South African champion Mike Carey.

Those black South African cycling athletes of the gold mines continued to race in teams at Rapport Toers, matching the efforts of some of the best of the white South Africans riders and of the European 'rebel riders'. Jack Ntseou was the first of the mine workers to win a stage, in 1979.

***

Racial interaction between black and white people in British cycling can be understood through the invitation given to African Caribbean people (the Windrush Generation) to migrate to and settle on the British Isles as citizens of Great Britain. The call from the British government was in seeking support to contribute in the work to rebuild the nation following World War Two (1939-1945).

It seems cordial welcomes were often given to Windrush Generation cyclists. British Oundle Wheelers club man Philip Ashbourn, for instance, fondly remembers his African Caribbean team-mate Barry Parkes.

Crack Cyclists Coming.

CONTINENTAL RECORD BREAKERS TO VISIT SOUTH WALES.

Considerable interest is being taken in the visit of three crack Continental cyclists to Carmarthen and Pontypridd next week. Piard, of France, the ex-amateur champion of the world, will be met by Heller, the champion of Austria, and Ibron Germain, the coloured crack of America, and rival of the great Major Taylor.

Ibron Germain (Nigger No. 2)

At the present time there are five niggers racing in Europe, but whether a new Major Taylor will be produced it is hard to say. Ibron Germain has been re-christened by the racing boys in Paris "Nigger No. 2," for the simple reason that he ranks as second to Major Taylor. "Nigger No. 2" will make his first trip to Great Britian during the Whitsuntide holidays. He was born at St. Pierre (Martinique) 22 years ago, and took a trip to France in 1901. He commenced riding as a professional right away, and when one Sunday afternoon he romped away with a first-class handicap from the best of company, the track managers thought they had found a new star. Last year he took a trip to Spain, where he won the Grand Prix at Vigo, and afterwards secured the paced Grand Prix at Lisbourne. During the latter part of last season he toured the South of France, and won the Grand Prix at Marseilles. Germain stands 5ft. 6in. and scales 9st. 6lb. He can speak four languages fluently.

A Welsh Evening Express article on Germain Ibron from 18th May 1907

We both lived in Stamford where there were few black people at the time [the 1950s]. Barry could perhaps have been the only one. We trained and raced together, and my parents were always pleased to see him for tea with his white girlfriend. Looking back to those days my memory is that all my club mates welcomed him and took extra care to make sure that cycling was as enjoyable for him as it was for us. Barry came from the West Indies which then had a great reputation for producing world standard cyclists, mainly on the track, to match their athletes and cricketers. Sadly, Barry died a few years later but I always think of him with great affection – [he was my] first black friend. I am sure my experience is not unique.

Another of the original migrants of the Windrush Generation was the Trinidadian racing cyclist Clyde Rimple. He decided to settle in London in 1958 after representing his country at the Empire Games in Cardiff. Rimple's arrival on the British cycling scene appeared to be warmly welcomed according to *Coureur Sporting Cyclist*.

Clyde moved to Lee Green where, able to make a real home with new-found friends, he took to the bike with a little more heart. Joining the Cambrian Wheelers [he] trotted round a few local races and took the club mile race at Charlton Sports.

Rimple began to participate in road and track racing. In 1960 he joined the Royal Air Force, and it was his performance at the RAF Track Cycling Championships that same year which got him noticed for a bigger cycling opportunity, as the same 1961 article notes.

Clyde Rimple made the cover of Jock Wadley's Sporting Cyclist 1961

[When] 'Rimp' romped home in front of Aircraftman Karl Barton in the R.A.F. Five at Herne Hill, his sports officer, Flying Officer Bernard Wallbutton, and ex-Somerset Roader and enthusiast for all types of quick cycling, set things going for the release of Rimple on a very special mission. A mission to Rome in the month of August for a term of duty with the Antilles team for the 17th Olympiad.

There he raced in track events against the likes of Sante Gaiardoni, the world sprint champion who went on to win double gold medals in the 1,000 metres time-trial and the match sprint. He also raced against Tullio Campagnolo and Cino Cinelli, who would both go on to found world-leading bike brands.

Such exploits meant he was pictured on the front cover of *Coureur Sporting Cyclist* in January 1961. Perhaps no British-based black racing cyclist had ever been highlighted in this way to the world of cycling. His welcome to and inclusion in the British cycling scene represented the inspiring possibilities that social and racial integration in the sport could bring to all. So why, 60 years after his success and over a century since the pioneering careers of the likes of Major Taylor and Kittie Knox, are there still so few recognised black champion cyclists? To what extent have times really changed for the black cyclist?

CHAPTER 2

HOW DID YOU GET INTO IT?

PERHAPS IF I HAD SEEN A MAGAZINE WITH A BLACK CYCLIST ON THE FRONT – MAURICE BURTON OR RUSSELL WILLIAMS OR NELSON VAILS RACING IN THEIR PRIME – I COULD HAVE BEEN INSPIRED BY THEM

MARLON LEE MONCRIEFFE

It wasn't seeing or knowing about a black cyclist that brought me into the sport. It was a photograph of the Spanish rider Miguel Induráin on the front cover of the May 1994 issue of *Cycle Sport*. That photo raised my interest in cycle racing to a different level. It was his smiling grimace; the cut in the muscle; the sweat; the black glasses; the Banesto cap; the yellow jersey. Perhaps if I had seen a magazine with a black cyclist on the front – Maurice Burton or Russell Williams or Nelson Vails racing in their prime – I could have been inspired by them. But Induráin was the leading light at the time. The contemporary sporting paragon gets the greater attention of the novice. Seeing, feeling and dreaming connects with who is doing the best at what you want to do. It doesn't matter if he or she is black or white.

It was summer and the Tour de France was on television. From time to time I had watched it, but I became more and more interested as I became a regular bike rider, particularly enamoured by my new idol Induráin and his battles with Tony Rominger.

At work, meanwhile, I had got talking to another cyclist. I'd met Mick a few times when riding home from Bermondsey. We used to race any other cyclist that got in our way, jumping traffic lights and racing to our imaginary finish line by the Clapham South tube station, where our routes home diverged.

Mick told me about the racing he was involved with at his club, and said they were looking for younger fellas to join. I was 20. I had other things on my mind that were appealing. I was not fully sold. But I had always loved sport and was pretty much always at the centre of it when I was at school. So I listened.

A guy called Stuart often joined in our conversations. He was another keen cyclist and talked about his racing bike, all the gears and kit on it. Of the two of us only Mick really understood, but I stayed in the conversation.

Stuart talked about how much he loved watching the Tour de France; about how he and his wife, who was Irish, were fans of Stephen Roche in particular and how they had been to Paris and the Avenue des Champs-Élysées to see the finale of the Tour in 1987 and how great it was to be there.

These cycling conversations became regular, and so did my burn ups on the bike with Mick through the streets of Bermondsey and Lambeth on the way home from work. All this enthusiasm planted a seed in my mind. I wanted to go and see the Tour for myself. So, I went to Paris and to go and watch my first bike race – the final stage of the 1994 Tour de France.

I persuaded my brother, Matthew, to come over with me. We watched the penultimate stage, a time trial, from our hotel. The next day we travelled on the Metro and stepped out on to the Champs-Élysées. I had never seen a road so wide. It was all dressed up in the *Tricolore*. We did not really know which way to walk. Just sort of looked at each other and followed our noses.

We wandered around taking in the atmosphere and ended up hanging around by the Place de la Concorde. The July sun was beating hot on us. We began to dehydrate. We had run out of money and only had enough to pay for our train fare to the airport.

Matthew managed to get himself a can of Coca-Cola from a young boy who was selling them to the people out of his cooler box.

That kept us going. The crowds gathered on the pavement and began
to block our view of the empty boulevard. So we shifted on, further
down the avenue. At one point I remember we were going to bail out.
But, no, we hung on.

It must have been about three or four hours before the circus
arrived. Then all of a sudden it began. The rushing noises. Car after
car; float after float; motorcycles. Cars with bicycles on rooftops.
Then silence for a short while, and then another lot of engines;
the passing of motorcycles; team cars with bikes; a car with a man
standing up, emerging from the sunroof, and then there they were,
the peloton, flashing around the corner with the Banesto team on the
front. I spotted Induráin. Yellow jersey, the cap, black sunglasses, led
by a team-mate looking serious on the front, almost like a bodyguard,
whilst the rest of his team followed, and then the peloton as part of
the parade. They came closer to where we were standing. Then they
were right next to us, and for a split second I was right in that
photo on the front cover of that magazine.

The peloton flashed by, all so smooth, no heavy breathing, a few
grimaces, no-one dying, all making racing the bike look so easy.
Then, more cars with bikes on top flew by and around and around
they all went, lap after lap. I had experienced the world of
professional cycling upfront and real.

**

My Jamaican-born mother noticed that I was getting into it. "Marlon.
Dem bicycle business. Me no really agree wid dem ting yu no."

She saw me going out on the bike early in the morning, every day,
in all seasons, rain or shine. She also saw me, more than once, return
home with cuts and bruises over my body from being smashed off
by half asleep car drivers. Her concern was more about the danger
of me riding the bike on the open roads with traffic, and the
possibility of hostile drivers.

My mother wasn't the only one to worry. In the 1970s, Maurice
Burton had similar conversations with his Jamaican-born father.

My dad saw it like: 'That bwoy need fe
have a trade. Get out deh, an tek a trade.
Dat likkle ting im is doing. Look at dat
bwoy. That bwoy still a ride dat bicycle?
Is about time you pack up dem bicycle
ting. What! You still a ride dat bicycle?
At dis age?' That was the kind of thing
that I got from my dad.

Despite being checked by his father, <u>Maurice's</u> desire to ride a bicycle was a force that he could not shake off, leading him to make an impulsive decision.

I wanted a bike because I used to lay in bed at night dreaming about riding a bike. But I did not have a bike. And so I took things into my own hands a bit. I got myself a bike that I had found in a front garden that was a bit wrecked. It had been involved in an accident, and I resurrected the bike and rode that bike.

In the early days, there was Dexter, my cousin. He lived in North London and I lived in South London. Anyway, what

used to happen between us was during the school holidays, I used to phone Dexter and then we used to meet at Blackfriars Bridge and we used to go off, riding for the day. We would go off somewhere and see things all around London. Dexter was the first person that I used to ride with a lot when I was a young fella.

The school that I went to was called Roger Manwood School. The guys that I used to hang around with were older than me and I knew that they went to Herne Hill Velodrome with the school. One of the reasons for me wanting to join that school, a big interest for me, was that when we got to a certain age we could go to Herne Hill Velodrome and race. Yeah, I liked that idea. It was as if that was my destiny, to ride a bike. Yes, very much so. I would say even from the very first time I went to Herne Hill Velodrome. We did not actually ride on the track on the day. We sat up in the grandstand. The man who was in charge of it all was a man called Bill Dodds. He said: 'From here, from this point here, you can go to the Olympic Games.' That was all that I needed to know at that point, because I thought: 'This is the place where I need to be.'

Herne Hill Velodrome in South East London, home to the Velo Club de Londres (VCL), was also a space of wonder for another young black rider. <u>Russell Williams</u> was living with his parents nearby and, after being invited to go along to a holiday club with his friend, he found himself walking into his own heaven.

The first thing I remember was the big difference between the Loughborough Junction area where we lived and the Herne Hill area. Herne Hill had beautiful houses. We walked down this beautiful street and suddenly there was this little entrance, and there it was, it opened, and there was this beautiful cycling track, Herne Hill.

We got there in the morning. There were other kids, about 40 or 50 of them, and all this action going on with people riding around the track. So we introduced ourselves. I think we had to pay something like 10 or 20 pence to take part in the class. I remember it ran from 10am to 12 noon: then a lunch break and then the next session from 1pm to 4pm. I remember during the whole morning we were not allowed on the cycling track. Instead we had to go through tuition about being on fixed wheel bicycles; every time you move looking over to the right. You know, I just really wanted to get on the track.

Eventually, we got on it in the afternoon, and it was great. I loved it. We had all sorts of racing we could do – three-lap races, one-lap sprints. It was the prizes that I remember as well. They were out of date mini-Mars Bars. Also, ice-cream cornets. They were out of date as well. But as a kid, at that time anyway, you think: 'Yes. Gimme some of that!' Anyway, we raced all afternoon, and it was great.

I was told about the training programme on Saturday mornings. So I started to do those. I remember small things that seemed weird to me, like the older boys who were aged around 14 and 15 riding with shaved legs. I was about 11 at that point and I remember speaking to some of them during the lunch break and them saying: 'Yeah, we shave our legs.' I remember thinking: 'What's all this about?' They all had the track mitts as well, the little gloves without finger covering. I remember after a few days of seeing that I took a pair of old gardening gloves that my father had and cut the fingers off from those. I took those up to the track cycling sessions and I thought: 'Yes! I'm part the team now.'

Charlotte Cole-Hossain knows the draw of that velodrome too, though she didn't have parental scepticism to deal with – quite the opposite.

My dad was a racing cyclist during his late teens and mid-20s. His brother rode as well, so cycling was in their family. He took me, my brother and my sister to the track and he would do some races. When we got slighter older, when I was about seven or eight years old, he decided to take me to Herne Hill Velodrome for us to have a go.

The first time, it was just my brother and me who did the riding and we really enjoyed it. I was very scared at first, just like most kids are, but we kept going and slowly became more and more familiar with the track.

From that, we started to go out on mountain bike rides, and we started to do things, but got slightly more into track cycling. Yes, it was mostly from him, both he and his brother were keen racers when they were younger.

Russell had parental support too.

My parents were 'keen as mustard' for me becoming an athlete in cycling. I am their only child and because we lived in South London, it was a hub of cycling activity with racing going on at Herne Hill, Crystal Palace, and later over in East London when the Eastway circuit opened.

My parents used to love coming over to the track to watch me race. It was a good little gig for them. My father used to drive me to races on a Sunday and we would go all other the place if I needed to race on the road somewhere. My parents were supportive. Having bikes in those days, even back then, it was a very expensive thing.

While Maurice Burton might have had parental doubts to deal with, his own son – Germain Burton – talks of the cultural capital inherited from his father's involvement in cycling.

I grew up in the sport and in the trade. I got involved in cycling through my dad. I have been involved since I was about nine years old. I actually first went out properly on a road bike with my dad and we rode a tandem. That was to help me to keep up with all of the other riders that my dad was riding with at the time. I did that for two summers, with not much in between apart from riding into school sometimes.

It was when I was 12 when I came off the tandem and on to my own road bike. I started riding with my dad and his club De Ver Cycles. We rode out from Streatham in London to the countryside in Kent and over into Surrey. I really loved it.

At that stage, my dad sat me down and said to me that if I really wanted to and I worked at it, he thought that I could do really well as an athlete.

That was really all I needed to hear. Ever since that point, after school finished, I'd tear it home on my bike in the summer, dash in, get changed and head straight out and be out on my bike for three hours, sometimes alone, sometimes with other people. When I was about 14 years old or so, I mostly rode alone. But I also rode quite often with my friend called Matt Watson who has always been one of my best mates. I used to go out with the De Ver Club riders, most of whom were a lot older than me. They were adults.

Before all of this, it was actually my mum who taught me how to ride a bike at a park just around the corner from us in Norbury. She used to inspect the ground for glass and clear it away with a broom and then she would hold the back of the bike and then when I was able to get the balance for myself, that was it. She'd count out laps and I'd be going around for ages and ages. That is my earliest memory of riding a bike.

I guess naturally, it was always going to be that way. I think with me and my siblings Robert and Grace, we all took a liking to cycling. But for me, it became part of my life very much.

My dad has been my biggest mentor. I got strong guidance and support from him in my riding and racing. I got a lot of discipline from my dad.

But I developed strong discipline and work ethic. My dad helped me there.

When I was younger, I used to go out for training and just batter myself to bits, just riding as hard as I could for two or three hours. I just loved riding my bike and riding my bike fast. He pulled me in a bit, so I didn't get carried away too much when I was younger.

When I started racing, I had my dad to help me with how to think about racing tactically and various things that I did not perhaps get the grip of initially. So I had him there to offer guidance at different events. Mental toughness, all of that.

But also it was about being able to enjoy the sport. I got that from him. I think it is all about enjoying the sport really. But with cycling, there are times when you are training really hard and it's not all laughing and joking. Sometimes it's about going out for hours in the rain or even in the snow, day in and day out, and that's not easy.

The motivation to succeed was always from me. My dad was there, and he would say: 'If this is what you want to do, it's not going to be easy...' and so on. He has been there and done it and so he helped me to see that. If anything, rather than him pushing me into it, I appreciated and learnt for myself that it was what I wanted to do.

In a sport like cycling, especially these days when there is so much attention to detail needed, you really have to put all of your time into it, especially if you want to make a living out of it.

Tre Whyte shares his reflections on the support he received from his family unit in making cycling part of their lifestyle.

I have got two brothers and a sister. They all took up BMX cycling after me. My dad took it up and began to ride and race BMX as well. At one point, my sister was ranked national number two, my dad was number four and I was ranked number two. My younger brother has been the British BMX champion 10 times. My older brother has been the British BMX champion. The support we had to get where we are was unreal. I mean, my dad quit his football. My mum would do whatever she could do in supporting us at the races. She was forever shouting out support and encouragement. We could always hear her. People used to call her 'The Mouth of the South'. My nan used to borrow money so that we could get to races, which were every month, all around England. So, no holidays.

So there was a point when it was all of us, the entire Whyte family, turning up at BMX races together for their individual events. There would be five or six of us in my dad's Vauxhall Zafira, with bike racks all over the car to get us to the races all around the country. People in BMX started to get to know our names.

French rider Grégory Baugé has also spoken of the importance of fatherly encouragement.

When I started, he was hesitant because I'd already been doing football for a while. When I said I wanted to take up cycling, there was the question of getting a [racing] licence to sort out, which was fairly expensive. Then we had to buy a bike. I had to justify myself. And that's how it started. But from the day I started, my dad always supported me, accompanied me to races and took me on all the long journeys. He was always there beside me.

Baugé's compatriot Kévin Reza started riding a bike at just four years old, encouraged by his father. Reza attended the CSM Puteaux cycling school as a child alongside his three siblings and went on to become a two-time national champion in the under-11 category (poussin which literally translates as 'chick'). He took his first title at seven and his second at eight.

Marie-Divine Kouamé Taky also speaks of support from her father.

He has always been my mentor. He has always supported me and encouraged me since my beginnings in cycling.

Justin and Cory Williams are others who come from a family of cycling champions. Their father Calman was the major influence on their uptake of bike racing. He rode at national and international level for Belize and as a Pan-American Games competitor. And their uncles raced professionally in Belize, winning the renowned Cross-Country Cycling Classic on multiple occasions. Justin and Cory were immersed regularly in family chats that reflected on those family stories of victory. Still, Justin Williams recounted the tough initiation to the sport given by his father.

My dad has always ridden a bike. My parents are from Belize, and in Belize it is a massive sport. I had been looking for a way to connect with my dad, because we did not have much in common. I tried working on cars with him. I tried having meaningful conversations with him. And nothing was working. So. One winter, one Californian winter, [Dad] had his bike on the trainers. So. I just decided to test my luck. And it was like a known thing: 'You don't touch my dad's bike.' But I just had to test my luck. It was like: 'Maybe if I ride a bike, we will have some quality father and son time.'

And I jumped on the bike and he just kind of just looked at me. So, I kept riding on the trainer, and it took him two months to take me outside and actually ride on the road. I'd spent two months on this trainer indoors, and then finally it was like: 'Alright. I'll take you out on the road for a ride.' And he took me out on a 70-mile ride. And on the way back, we were like 20 miles away from home. And I just cracked. I was cramping. I am dying. I have no glycogen in my body. I pulled over to the side of the road.

When I first started riding, I used to wear boxers under my bibs. He hated it.

41

Tre Whyte of Great Britain, the defending world BMX champion, ahead of the 2015 UCI BMX World Championship finals in Zolder, Belgium

He told me not to do it three times. I was uncomfortable. I did not want to wear tights. Especially where I was from. It was like: 'Come on, man!' So he like pulled my shirt up to give me a massage, trying to get the cramp out. And I had boxer shorts on. He was like: 'Dude! I've told you not to wear boxer shorts under your bibs.' And he left me. He left me on the side of the road.

For the Williams brothers, cycling was a means to set goals and aspirations for themselves outside their tough neighbourhood upbringing, as Justin recounted.

I grew up in south central Los Angeles, where there is not a ton of opportunities. I think the statistic is that one in every three black males will end up in prison at some point in their life, so the odds were already stacked against me. I had a clear vision of that early, and I did not want to grow up and be like everyone else. Cycling was the perfect outlet for me to step outside of that bubble.

And of the hostilities in the neighbourhood that he grew up around, Williams continues.

I remember it being unpredictable. A lot of gang members in the community and kids selling drugs on the street. Other than our time riding bikes, my parents kept us inside, focused on studying. They didn't trust us to go out, which feels justified now. You could easily be caught in the wrong place and end up dead or in jail. I remember bullet holes in our street sign. I don't know what I would have done without a bike.

Navigating the tough neighbourhoods and finding an escape through cycling is reflected in the early experiences of Rahsaan Bahati. At 11 years old, he was talent spotted by his sixth grade teacher, Reggie Garmon. At the Olympic Carson Velodrome, Bahati found a place of solace; somewhere he could express himself away from his Compton, Los Angeles neighbourhood.

That [the velodrome] was home for me for a long time. If I was not at the track, I was literally at home. If I was not at home I was at the track. It was not until I was about 13, maybe 13 and half, when it was like: 'Man, I really like this bike thing.'

Bahati's parents helped him make that realisation into a formal commitment.

Cycling was an afterschool programme. It was a form of punishment. I was running track, playing football, and playing baseball. My dad said: 'You need to make a decision. You are doing all these sports. I am running around town. Pick one.' And without hesitation, I chose cycling.

I go back to my parents. They were the foundation for the decisions I made. When it came to doing the right thing, it came down to their parenting.

Bahati also says the discipline of cycling provided him with a life education that schooling could perhaps never offer.

I didn't shake the hand of somebody who wasn't black until I was about 14 or 15 years old. That may seem to be a little weird or strange. But you grow up in Compton, Compton is pretty much black. My school was predominantly black. You know, black or Hispanic. So who else are you going to communicate with? That was my bubble. So, cycling really took me outside of that bubble. It took me all over the place and that is what really shaped me. That moving around. That travel. It's bigger than an education at an institution in my opinion. I had acquaintances and friends from Compton who were losing loved ones every day to gun violence. Growing up in a situation like that, in an environment like that. When you have something like a bike race, it doesn't stress me out. Growing up where I grew up, bike racing was nothing but an escape from the concrete jungle. Cycling and racing for me was just a way to get away. I never had stress. I knew that there was a bigger picture.

In the sometimes-tough neighbourhoods of South London, are the homes of the majority of successful black British cyclists. It's where

Maurice, Russell, Charlotte, Germain and I all grew up. We are
all children and grandchildren of the South London Windrush
Generation. Charlie Reynolds; brothers Gary and Wayne Llewellyn,
Tre and Kye Whyte and Quillan and Tian Isidore – all developed
their bike skills there too, inner-city skate parks providing the
grounding of their future national and international successes in
BMX. Tre Whyte describes the scene.

I grew up in the South-East of London, in
the Peckham Rye area. I started riding
BMX at around the age of nine. I was
really into it, without even knowing that
BMX was an Olympic sport. That is just
what I wanted to do. When it got to the
age where you had to put all the work in
yourself, that is how it had to be for me.

Peckham was a tough area. There were
lots of gangs that used to hang around.
If I were out there doing my sprints and if
I were in a particular area, I could not be
out there late at night practising. I could
be robbed. But I knew enough people in
the area to get by alright. You know,
I did not find it a problem speaking with
people in those gangs. But I never really
wanted that gang life. I kind of saw that.

Charlie Reynolds' reflections give a vivid perspective of a young boy
taking all opportunities from cycling to rise above the circumstances
of some tough early years.

My life has not been straightforward.
I am the youngest of my siblings. As
young children, we were placed into
the care system and were split up. I had
to live in children's homes mainly in the
Gloucestershire area. It was very tough.
I grew up with no loving. But care home
was the place where I started putting
bikes together for myself.

When I was back in London, when
I was around eight or nine years old,
I would love going out and doing jumps,
skidding down the road. It was a passion
within me at a young age.

As soon as I could compete and be in
a race, that was me, I was there. It is
unfortunate that my parents never ever
saw me race.

Being in and out of the care home was
a trying time. In 1981 in London, when
the skate park turned up in our
neighbourhood, I was discovered by
a man called Ken Floyd. He was based
at my first team – Brixton BMX Club.
Ken was a black man who looked out
for black children in difficult situations.
Ken used to arrange for a minibus, and he
would take us all to races. Without Ken's
influence, there are a lot of black riders
that would never have got anywhere in
the sport. In the early 1980s, he actually
led the building of the BMX track behind
Brixton Police Station. When I went to
race with Ken and the guys, I was spotted
by Edwardes Cycles of Camberwell.
They saw me and said: 'Bloody hell!
Do you want to come and ride for us?'
They obviously saw something in me.

Some black British champion riders accessed the sport and developed the beginnings of their riding and racing away from an inner-city upbringing. David Clarke is also a grandchild of the Windrush Generation but his early life was forged in the Midlands, in Burton-on-Trent. He remembers being influenced by his grandfather's love of cycling, and says receiving that inheritance at a young age shaped his mindset and ambition to become a racer.

My grandad, Keith Lee, was quite into cycling. That is where I picked it up from. That is where I got the bug from originally. He was a reasonably good racing cyclist in his early 20s and then he stopped for a number of years. When he started again in his early 50s he wasn't racing competitively but he would be riding over 100 miles on a Sunday and he'd be out three or four times a week, averaging around 50 miles each day.

He was a builder by trade. I think he did a job where he agreed that the guy would part pay him with a brand new bike. So there was always this bike in my grandad's house sitting in the hallway. I guess that bike was something that I looked up to when I was younger. You know, we would watch the Tour de France and I had always assumed that I would be racing on that bike at some point.

Once I decided that I was going to be a professional cyclist, I was only ever going to be a professional cyclist. Even at the age of, say, four or five, I was not easily swayed out of that idea.

My grandad was always keen. I learnt to ride on a little racing bike. My grandad bought that from France. It had 20-inch wheels. There was nothing of that type in the UK at that time. I never had stabilisers on anything. My grandad would run behind me, holding my saddle. It seems almost bizarre and, if anything, impossible to think about it, but I remember we rode out to the local hospital and back which has got to be a good 10- to 12-mile loop, maybe further, with my grandad holding the back of my saddle.

I have got one brother who is two-and-a-half years younger than me and he cycled until his mid-teens. Me, my brother, and my grandad used to cycle a lot together when I was younger. There were a few others on our road that we used to cycle with. There was a little lad called Robert Malcolm, he used to cycle a bit. But never really anyone else with us on a regular basis. We used to ride a loop around to Tamworth on Tuesdays – my grandad used to have Tuesdays off work.

When it was the school holidays, we used to go out for 30 or 40 miles. When I was 10, I did the Cycling Tourists Club (CTC) 100 miles ride in eight hours. My brother did the same ride when he was nine years old, to be fair. The first time we did it, he did the 50 miles ride in four hours and he would have been eight then. We did the Lung Foundation sponsored charity ride which was 50 miles, and we would have been five and seven years old at the time. We did not join a cycling club until after the Lung Foundation ride.

Mark McKay is another champion cyclist who did not come from a British city background. He accessed the sport as an 18-year-old, shifting his athletic abilities from high level football to cycling. He pursued his goals without much family support, developing a path for himself through local racing enthusiasts.

Looking back, I can see that my bike racing ability developed at a good pace despite the fact that I did not really have much direction in making cycling a career as such.

I didn't come from a cycling family and my hometown of Northampton was certainly no hotbed of bike racing. So getting the right influences to direct me towards a professional career never materialised. Some local people in the sport could see that I was making solid progress, but in the late 80s and early 90s, there didn't seem to be the level of professional coaching advice available that there is nowadays, to offer much in the way of structured training advice for instance.

What is clear is that family support makes an enormous difference to black people who want to get involved in the world of cycling. Trinidadian rider Teniel Campbell has said regularly biking with her brother helped develop her racing career. Shanaze Reade has spoken about the influence of her uncle and cousins in giving her access to the world of BMX. But family support isn't a given. Outliers such as Charlie Reynolds were able to find strong mentors who supported their desire to pursue a journey in the sport. For riders like Maurice Burton and me there was some caution from our parents in taking up cycling, but we pursued our desires regardless.

CHAPTER 3
WHAT THE FUCKING HELL ARE YOU DOING HERE WITH US?

WE WERE THE ONLY BLACK CYCLISTS – THEY CALLED US MONKEYS AND TOLD US TO EAT OUR BANANAS. AT THE TIME I DIDN'T REALISE IT WAS RACISM. I WAS NOT EVEN AWARE OF BEING DIFFERENT

MARIE-DIVINE KOUAMÉ-TAKY

Marie-Divine Kouamé Taky, UCI junior
500m track cycling world champion 2019

My first bike race was a 10-mile time trial. My ears were full of an airy droning noise composed of trucks and cars swooshing by me at 60 miles an hour. I plodded on; my legs screaming at me. Then an even louder blast in my ear: "You've got to hurt!!! You gotta hurt!!! You gotta hurt!!" I looked up and across. The rider who had screamed flicked his head at me and flashed by. "You gotta hurt!!" he bellowed once more, gesticulating with his arm. He was all red and pumped up as he screamed at me from under his aero-helmet on his carbon bike with tri-bars, disc wheel, skinsuit. I was on my steel-framed racing bike, drop bars, dreadlocks, baggy kit. He turned his head, and pedalled hard, trying to get away from me on the dual carriageway. His cry seemed to be a strange mixture of contempt and encouragement.

The droning noise continued. I was on the limit. I tracked him to the turn. I did not let him out of my sight. It was the same man who was glaring at me earlier in the car park. It wasn't in a welcoming way, but more of what I could sense was a disdainful: "What the fucking hell are you doing here with us?" stare.

My world had changed when we pulled into that car park hidden away within the North Downs in Surrey. Car boots were open. Bikes leaned on the side of cars. Road bikes, tandems, tricycles. There were lots of older white men: some bent down fiddling with bikes, others scattered around in their red, white and black kit, heading in and out of the woods with urgency. Some walked with curved backs. Some had blue-veined, skinny and bowed white legs. Some wore old-fashioned black laced cycling shoes with their white socks. Some had Edwardian walrus-style moustaches. There was a buzz, a vibe in preparation for action.

Amongst all of this, some older women were busily getting a tea table ready. Silver urn, teacups, home-made cakes, checked tablecloth. This was an English garden party occurring in the Surrey woods on a Thursday evening with the Redmon Cycling Club. I had entered a strange subculture with much to observe, not least the idiosyncratic appearances of cyclists fixed to a particular era, dress codes, pre- and post-race rituals, and behaviours.

After the race, whilst he was in the middle of changing out of his kit, the cyclist who shouted at me came over and carried on. "This is not a park ride you know. You were sitting on your bike looking around at the hills and everything."

"Was I?" I thought. I looked at him. I politely pretended to listen to what he was saying as he went on. I carried on dismantling my bike as he continued. He eventually walked off back to his car to finish changing out of his racing kit.

I grew up on a predominantly white council estate in Roehampton in South-West London. I had lived long enough amongst white people to detect those who felt uncomfortable with the black presence. Maurice Burton had the same sixth sense in his early experiences of riding with his first club.

I became a member of the VCL (Velo Club de Londres). Well I guess there are a lot of people of colour in the VCL now. But at the time that I went in there, it was only me. I used to ride with some of those guys, and some were OK. I remember going out riding with a few of them one day, and I rode behind them for like 60 miles, and they never spoke to me. I think it may have been because of the colour of my skin. I just rode with them, and that was it.

Maurice's reflection chimes with Rahsaan Bahati's more direct response concerning his experience of anti-blackness on some of his first club rides.

I have been on training rides where I have had older adults who did not like me because, one, the colour of my skin, and two, I was better than them. This is as a kid, having a white guy in his 40s tell me to get off a ride.

Grégory Baugé spoke about the racist abuse directed towards him and his family at the beginning of his cycling career.

I'd hear things and so would my family. I didn't hear stuff so often from the young riders, but when you looked them in the face, you could see what they were thinking. When a black rider wins, the person you beat can get annoyed. My parents told me not to take any notice, not to say anything. They brought me up well and so that's what I did. Yes, it hurts, but on the other hand, it just made me push the pedals even harder.

This unwanted attention that a person with a black skin attracts in a majority white world is common in cycling. David Clarke shares some of his thoughts concerning the neighbourhood environment he grew up in and the cycling clubs he became a member of.

I joined the local CTC and progressed to Mercia Cycling Club which was a local cycling club. There was not anybody of a similar ethnicity to me in that club. In Newall itself, there was not anybody of a similar ethnicity anyway. I was always conscious of it. You know, there was a fair bit of racism in those times. It was not something that you were always able to forget.

To have to wake up every day with the immediate thought that you may face hostilities, hate and even physical violence in cycling from white people simply because of having a skin colour that does not match theirs was the reality of Major Taylor. But to what extent has this level of racism continued in cycling? Maurice Burton shared with

me an account of how his friend Joe Clovis, another black rider, was dragged away from the sight of spectators by white cycling rivals after a race at Crystal Palace and assaulted.

There was a bit of an argument off the bike. Two of the guys held Joe whilst another laid into him. I was not there. But if I were, it would have been a different matter. They really would have seen me.

That was in the 1970s. But what about today? Nicholas Dlamini, a black South African cyclist, has spoken of the physical mistreatment he has witnessed.

It is true that there has been a lot of incidents of racism in the peloton. I've seen it happening to the African guys. I've seen it happen to Natnael Berhane. We were racing up a climb and it was crunch time. Natnael was about 20 metres ahead of me, and there was this one rider moving up. He came alongside Natnael and just pushed him straight off the road. I looked at that and I thought: 'You can't do that.' But Natnael didn't mind it. I think it's happened so many times to him that he doesn't even take it into account anymore. But I saw what it was like. It wasn't cool. I think the guy just looked at him and thought:

57

The French professional Kévin Reza is arguably the most successful black road racing cyclist. He has been a pro since 2007 and has completed five Grand Tours including three Tours de France

'You're a black guy. You're not supposed to be here anyway. I need to go past, so I'm just going to push you.' Those small things.

The violence of racism towards the black cyclist is apparent mostly through verbal taunts from white riders. In the 2014 Tour de France, Kévin Reza was racially abused by the Swiss rider Michael Albasini. Reza was the target of racist abuse again from the Italian rider Gianni Moscon during the third stage of the Tour de Romandie in 2017. Reza has reflected on these encounters.

At first, I thought: 'No, it is not possible that it is 2017 and there is still that kind of talk.' Anyone can get carried away during a race, because it goes so fast, we get tired. There are words we say when we are upset, not-so-kind names, insults, and all that, but we do not go beyond that. To get carried away in this case like that, to use a slur, I really didn't let it pass and I wanted to fix it myself [with him], but unfortunately, after the finish line there were cameras, photos taken, and it made the same noise as in 2014 and it got out of hand.

Speaking about Reza's treatment, the American cyclist Erik Saunders said.

When African riders started to compete in the Tour de France it was shocking to people. When you see a black man on a bike there are different kinds of reactions – it's a novelty (at best) or it's a sign of something that's coming, something that threatens their position. People see you where they think you don't belong and they ask: 'What's the agenda?'

At the 2014 Tour of Spain, Douglas Ryder – team principal for the African MTN-Qhubeka – recounted how, when his riders were trying to bring one of their black team-mates to the front of the bunch in the mountains "one of the biggest teams in the world... shouted: 'You guys don't belong here, fuck off to the back of the bunch.'" Mark McKay has a similar memory.

I remember being in a race in Belgium or Holland and facing racist abuse in the peloton from one or two Dutch riders, I think simply because they had never experienced racing against non-white opponents before.

And so has Germain Burton.

There has been some racism. In Belgium when I was a junior rider I can remember I got some verbal abuse. Whether it is what some people call insidious racism, or whether it is outright racism, you know, in your face racism, it is out there.

Charlotte Cole-Hossain spoke of her experiences of being subjected to white-female gang violence when racing as a junior in the Netherlands.

There were a lot of complaints at the end of one race. All the Dutch girls kind of ganged up on me. One rider even accused me of pulling her hair during the race. It was unbelievable. I think it had to do with me looking different to all of them.

In that same event a couple years later, a team-mate of mine who was also of black parentage was called a nigger by a Dutch rider whilst racing. We obviously spoke to the judges and commissaires afterwards. They aimed to sort it out.

But you would have expected or hoped at least that somebody who does that in a race would get disqualified from the race because it is racial abuse.

But that young white rider, I am not sure whether he even got a telling off, because he was allowed to start the race the next day. I guess we stood out. When you have over 300 youth and junior riders at one event and only a few of them are mixed-race or with black heritage, it is easy to become a target.

What do all these racist incidents evidence? That, at all levels of the sport, there are still white racing cyclists who are incapable of figuring out a way to cope with the unfamiliarity of ethnic diversity in their sport and in their workplace. And so they abuse ethnic diversity through their ignorance.

The underlying attitude of racism permeates the culture of officialdom too. Joe Clovis, a contemporary of Maurice Burton, was regularly refused permission to race at Herne Hill on the basis his tubular tyres were not considered safe. His white friends could not believe this and so decided to test this 'rule' by bringing the same wheels for inspection by the same officials. They were granted permission to race.

As recently as 2012 – when Maurice Burton, along with a large group of his predominantly black British De Ver cycling team club mates, travelled to watch his son Germain race at the World Junior Road Race Championships – such racism from officials has still been on display.

We hired a large 20-seater coach for a group of us. We drove this thing over there. I will not forget what those officials did. When they saw us, they began laughing and talking about monkeys or something. It was out of order. For those officials around the podium area in their UCI blazers to be going on like that. I have a photograph of them. In this day and age! They should not be in the sport.

Marie-Divine Kouamé Taky has also experienced attempts by white people to diminish her through ugly racism.

When I was 11 years old, I took part in Trophée de France des Jeunes Cyclistes – it is a competition that brings together all the regions of France represented by two youth riders in each category.

I took part with my best friend Joris Inapogui, who is of Ivorian origin. We were the only black cyclists. When we were surrounded by the other children, they called us monkeys and told us to eat our bananas. These behaviours were produced in front of their parents, who said nothing.

We went to see our parents and they told us that it was on the bike that we were going to show them what we are capable of. At the time I didn't realise it was racism. I was not even aware of being different. It was at the age of 11, following these insults, that I understood racism.

The racial difference of being white in comparison to being black and seeing that divide of 'othering' framed by fictional characters is a deeply embedded cultural mindset on the European continent. In the Netherlands, white people often 'black up' during the Christmas season as the Black Pete, an extremely unattractive but at the same time mild and generous assistant of the white-bearded Santa Claus. Black Pete is known for handing out presents and sweets to young people as Maurice recounts.

I was once mistaken for Black Pete by some young children when I was racing in Rotterdam. '*Kijken! Het is Zwarte Piet!*' they would say. It did not really bother me. They did not know any better. In my racing and training rides some riders used to say: 'Watch out for the Zwarte!'; you know, watch out for the black man. That is how it was. That's how they were.

Tre Whyte shares his feelings of surveillance when part of the British Cycling talent team at the National Cycling Centre.

My older brother Daniel was on the programme before me and he was treated differently by people. He eventually had to leave. So when I first moved up to Manchester to join the talent team, I felt like my [black] identity and my

background [coming from a council estate in Peckham, London] could create some barriers for me. Little things. Like, people would say that I 'drove a stolen car' and 'had it out there in the garage'. It was not stolen at all. I had people in positions of power calling me on the phone and telling me to 'get rid of that stolen car', or you are gonna be 'kicked off' [the talent team]. I sensed I was not liked very much. You know, I was like 18 going on to 19 years old at the time.

Tim Erwin's reflections on his experiences of being othered chime with what Tre encountered as the National Cycling Centre talent team interloper.

Being black [in a dominant white space] can feel like you are screaming into the void. We've said that these things happen, and then they happen again, and again, and again, but nothing changes. It [racism] is so ingrained in the culture. Like, the suspicion that comes with having a nice bike. I can remember taking my own bike into a shop in Louisiana, and getting asked: 'Did you steal this bike?' The average white person gets talked down to in shops a lot of times; the average black person gets talked down to and is assumed to be a criminal.

Christian Lyte can relate to that sense of shame and embarrassment unfairly imposed upon black riders who enter the white-dominated world of cycling. Like Tre, he was a member of the British Cycling talent team. And, like Tre, he felt marginalised.

I was with the talent team for two years and then it progressed to the Olympic Development Programme. [At that time] there were not any other cyclists like me; you know, of a similar ethnic identity. You do question it a bit. I think that there were some social and interactional barriers for me when I was at British Cycling. I think people already saw me as an outsider. You know, different to the normal [white] cyclist on the talent team. I did not have that face to fit if that makes sense. Most of the guys that were on the squad at the time were, you know, there were a few Yorkshire lads who were kind of like 'lad lads'; you know like typical sort of English lads. I just did not sort of get along with that, at the time.

The experiences of Tre and Christian chime with early career African American experiences, including those of Justin Williams.

The hardest part was probably the isolation. Feeling like you are not understood. People not really knowing how to deal with you. What is important to you, what troubles you.

66

<u>Rahsaan Bahati</u> had similar experiences.

[Being in] a predominantly white fraternity when with Team TIAA-CREF in 2016 meant I didn't fit in. That's what it felt like. The net effect of these constant reminders that you are an outsider is to make you think: 'Maybe I'm never going to belong, and I shouldn't be doing this.' That is the impact. Any black person who exists in a white space like cycling has to check a part of themselves at the door.

Rahsaan sums up the sense shared by so many others – that the black cyclist is made to feel as though he or she has committed an offence by turning up in the white-dominated world of bike riding. When black people enter cycling, they enter a space in which there is a privileged entitlement that comes with whiteness. They are made fully aware that their minority-ethnic identity makes them different. In turn, that rider carries the false perception of having committed an offence by bringing a black body into a white space.

CHAPTER 4
LET YOUR LEGS DO THE TALKING

Nelson Vails started out racing for New York's Team Toga Tempo in the early 1980s

AT THE EARLY STAGES OF BIKE MESSENGERS IT WAS GREAT MONEY. I DEVELOPED A VERY ACUTE SENSE OF AWARENESS ON THE BICYCLE IN THE CITY. NEW YORK CITY BIKE MESSENGERS ARE LIKE NO OTHER

NELSON VAILS

"I was club rider of the year in 1971. On Monday nights at Herne Hill Velodrome was the Track League, and I won it with 83 points against the second person who had 42 points. I won with nearly double points of the second rider. That's how it was from the very beginning. I only really raced at Herne Hill and at the Crystal Palace circuit because I didn't have the transport to get me to other places. I turned junior in my second year of racing and won the divisional championship in 1972. In 1973 I won the White Hope Sprint at Herne Hill. The national coach at that time was Norman Sheil. He was the world pursuit champion in 1955. I remember the first time I saw him watching me race; his eyes were popping out of his head. Norman took me under his wing. He said something that I will always remember: 'Let your legs do the talking'."
Maurice Burton

For me, time trials gave an opportunity to take part in open racing events in Surrey and Sussex. I remember how Sean Yates, David Akam and Tim Stephens would appear, calling themselves Team Clean – and, sure enough, they would clean up all the prize money. Here I was, a beginner racing cyclist on the same start sheet as professional cyclists, Grand Tour riders. I had seen Sean Yates racing on the Champs-Elysées back in 1994. Now he was here, in the flesh, in the makeshift race HQ of a school dinner hall, signing on to take part in a local time trial with the common man.

There was no lack of motivation from members of the Redmon Cycling Club. I remember one of the older guys telling me on a club ride: "You need to pull your finger out!" I really didn't have a clue as to what he was talking about. But I sensed it meant work harder.

I got my legs working well during the winter of 97/98. Maybe it was because I was in the final year of my university studies. I rode some 100 miler winter reliability rides that had been advertised in the back pages of *Cycling Weekly*. Mick said there would be some good riders in these. I didn't know much about who was who at the time, but the fast group that we rode was led by Tony Doyle and Rob Hayles, both pros. Mick told me to sit in at the back with him.

As Doyle and Hayles and the others chatted away at the front of this group of around 20 riders, we must have averaged around 28 mph in the cold, foggy January air. The ride started off in the Kingston upon Thames area and we rode through Surrey and Sussex and back. No hanging around. No nice coffee breaks. Three to four hours non-stop. Mick told me that he'd never seen me go so fast up the hills. I felt strong. But mainly I didn't want to be dropped and left out there alone on some unfamiliar country road looking for the nearest unfamiliar train station to get me home to London, as a few other riders had been. I enjoyed those rides. Twickenham CC also did the Findon Bash from Hampton Court train station to Bury Hill in West Sussex and back, at a similarly ruthless pace.

When the spring came, I took a holiday season job as a London bicycle courier. I was riding around 80 kilometres every day. I was paid for the amount of deliveries I made in a day, and I would beat the motorbike couriers to the jobs. I would ride from Roehampton to Wandsworth to Battersea to Chelsea to Piccadilly. Then all day around Central London. Waterloo Bridge, London Bridge, Tower Bridge, Clerkenwell, Oxford Street, Kings Cross, back to Soho, over to Albert Embankment drafting the lorries at 45 mph, then a final burn up to Wandsworth, and back home.

Nelson Vails also developed his bike handling skills as a bicycle messenger in a big city, and gives an interesting take on his multicultural interactions within the daily traffic.

To be a New York City bike messenger at the early stages of bike messengers, it was great money. I developed a very acute sense of awareness on the bicycle in the city. New York City bike messengers are like no other. You have them in Chicago, in San Francisco. Same style, but I think New York City is a melting pot of drivers of different nationalities – and all the different driving habits – and that helps to strengthen your bicycle skills.

Following his day of riding in New York City's ethnically diverse collection of car drivers, he'd head off to Central Park in the evenings, getting involved in racing with local cycling groups. All of this leg work paid off.

I was winning lots of local races, and then going to the track national championships in 1980 was a turning point for me. I didn't win but I had a good show. This launched me and gave me the opportunity to be on the USA Olympic development team. From that time it's the summer of 1982 at Trexlertown Velodrome that stands out. This put me on an international stage for racing.

It was me as a category 4 rider now racing with the elites and the professionals. I was able to hold my own. I was the young guy coming up, mixing into the professional scene and causing a stir. I took wins against Eric Heiden and Louis Garneau.

I raced in all the races: the scratch races, the sprints, all of the different distances. As a kid, and being enthusiastic, you know, the coach threw me in and I was like: 'What do I do?' And he was like: 'Just go! See what happens. Test yourself. If you lose, well, look at who are racing against. If you win? It's a big hurrah!' 40-50% of the time I would win or get second. But I would get second because I didn't know what I was doing at that age.

If I was going to do some time trialling then I needed a time trial bike. But there was no way I could afford to buy any of the expensive futuristic carbon bikes that the 10-miles-in-19-minutes-men of Team Clean were using.

I honestly didn't know where to start. One day, I ventured down to Pearson Cycles in Sutton to buy some inner tubes. Outside the front of the shop I clocked a Raleigh Dyna-Tech low profile time trial bike with a tag on it: 'For sale – £275.' I couldn't believe it. It had Reynolds tubing, tubular wheels, and compared to the steel load that I was riding, it was light as a feather.

Nelson Vails winning in front of a packed crowd at the Olympic Velodrome in Los Angeles 1984

I immediately stepped into the shop and spoke to Guy Pearson, the shop's owner. When I sat on the bike, my chin was almost scraping the ground. But I wanted it. I negotiated a price of £220.

I thought about how I could convert it to make it rideable. I put a mountain bike stem on it and used a bit of my student loan to buy a new Spinergy rear wheel. It was probably one of the fastest bikes I ever rode.

My aim was to bring my Thursday night 10-mile time trial time down to something respectable. I thought if I could do a 21 I would be going well. Another target for me at that point was to win the club's 10-mile time trial championship. Everyone in the club spoke about it as the big event held in August.

The week before the championship, I took the train down to Dorking from Clapham Junction for my regular Thursday night engagement. I rode over to the car park, signed on. I was ready. I took the win that night with a 21 ride. "Great ride, Marlon. Club championships next week," I remember Mick saying. I knew that. But I pretended it didn't matter.

When the championships rolled round, I repeated the same procedure as the week before. Train from Clapham Junction to Dorking, rode over to the sign on. It was going to be my night.

Grégory Baugé at the 2007 World
Championships in Palma de Mallorca

I knew the dual carriageway by now. I knew how to hurt in time
trials. The club secretary Jim Walsh and his wife Jean walked over
just before the start. "Fast evening tonight, Marlon. Go for it,"
Jim said. And I did. I got back to the car park to see the scoreboard.
I did it. I'd won.

I'd entered that world of cycling a few years prior as a novice racer
and now I had become a champion – well, at least in the eyes of the
people who had given me an opportunity to race.

***

The taste of victory. It is important to any novice racing cyclist.
It gives confidence and affirmation. <u>Grégory Baugé</u> reflected on his
first races and wins in cyclo-cross.

I started when I was nine. I learned
quickly and won my first cyclo-cross race
just six months later. It was at Conflans,
in the Yvelines region. Cyclo-cross is a
form of racing that I still love. I rode
cyclo-cross until I was 16.

I was 10 years old when I won that
first race. It was superb. Your first win
brings a special joy – seeing your family
there, your friends, all of them happy.
I didn't have a chance to raise my hands
in the air that time, but I won three

times in a row, riding in plimsolls.

I wasn't inspired by the track in the beginning. But things weren't going so well for me on the road. The races weren't going the way I wanted them to. So, I went to the track, just to see. That was when I was about 13 years old.

It was a sprint championship at the Cipale track in Paris – the national cadet championship. I really enjoyed it, and I came second. Even though I didn't win, it gave me a lot of pleasure. And that's how my track career started. I made my choice.

Rahsaan Bahati considers a pivotal race in his early career, when he started to believe in his ability.

The turning point for me was when I was 13 years old. I was put up in a race against a guy who was 18 years old. He was a national champion at the time for track sprinting. Just from watching bike racing, and from riding the track for a year and a half, I don't know what it was but I had a knack for paying attention to things. I was never as fast or as strong as some of the other older guys, but I could outsmart them.

I remember going to the bell lap and I was riding behind him. I remember thinking: 'Man! For about a second to two seconds he looks behind at me, and then he doesn't look at me. So, if he does

that going into turn two, if he looks at me, when he does that, I am going to dive down the track to see if I can catch him off guard.' Keeping in mind this is a big track: 333 metres; it's a long way home to finish from turn two at 13 years old going up against an 18-year-old with a bigger gear, what not.

Anyway. I smoked him. He had no idea that I was down the track on the black line and gone. He must have looked over his shoulder again and realised that I was not there. By the time he looked forward to see where I was, I was already coming out of turn three. The coaches there just went crazy.

Bahati gives the story of how he won the first of his 10 USA national championships.

I won my first national title on track, not on the road. It was the national junior championships. I was 15 years old, and this was in San Diego, in my home state. I had a big rival who came to take part from Trexlertown Velodrome, a kid called John Retseck. 'T Town' produces a lot of great riders for the track. It didn't matter what age the riders were. From 11 years old up to adults, they are all pretty good.

When the TT boys came into town, you knew it was business.

John was the same age as me – 15. But this guy was just the beast. At 15, I weighed around 135 pounds. I was maybe about 5ft 10 inches in height. John must have been around 5ft 5 inches, but at around 165 pounds of pure muscle. So he is a typical T Town racer, a little intimidating. I got second to him for

Charlotte Cole-Hossain at the Friends of Herne Hill Velodrome Youth Team Championships 2015

THESE WERE SERIOUS BOYS, WHO HAVE BEEN TRAINING REALLY HARD AND PROPERLY, WHILST I WAS STILL KIND OF DOING IT JUST FOR FUN AND I MANAGED TO STAY IN THERE WITH THEM

CHARLOTTE COLE-HOSSAIN

Germain Burton winning the 2010
Bec Hill Climb at the age of 16

three title races in a row. So here I am on the podium. I had three silver medals. John won all of those races.

My uncle was in town from Alabama. He saw me lose all three races. On the last day, my uncle was there on the rails watching, and he yells out across the track to me: 'I got $300 for you if you beat this boy!' at the top of his lungs.

The last race was the 30 laps scratch race. I am not sure if the money was the motivation. It was the last race of the championships. I wanted to give my all it. I won that race. I took home some money. But more importantly, I won my first national championships title. My win was a very fulfilling moment. Not only just to put the jersey on, but to beat another rider who seemed to be unbeatable. John and I eventually ended up as team-mates with Mercury Cycling.

Learning to lose is a painful but necessary step towards becoming a champion, as Justin Williams recalls.

I was a first-year junior. It was the track nationals in Pennsylvania at T Town. I had a race there the year before and I had got been pretty bad by Shane Klein. He was my arch-nemesis. He was from there. He is a really great guy. We were always good friends off the bike. But we fought to the death when we were on the bike. It was his home track, his backyard.

So that year, I showed up. I did the training. At this point I am 16 turning 17. I had only been racing since age 14.

I mean the first year that I started riding, I didn't do track racing at all. I didn't even try the track until it was my third year. So, I show up and I was going to be ruthless. I won the match sprint. It was great. It was just about outfoxing my opponent. I had a bit more fitness than Shane on the day, but we were pretty much evenly matched for speed.

In the Keirin it was the same thing. Strange thing was, the motor pulled off and then the race went to top of the track because everyone was just watching each other. It turned into a match sprint in the Keirin. We were coming into turn four with one lap to go at the top of the track. It is a 333-metre track. So, when somebody went, I took third wheel for a good leadout to the line. I kicked going into turn four. I came around and won that one. It was two down. It was great.

Something had changed in my mindset as to why I was doing this. It felt like people changed immediately on how they viewed me. It was a vibe. My words were given more importance in how they were received by people. It typically shows. Sometimes it is not the spoken word, it is body language. Sometimes it is about having people's attention when you say something. Having that respect. There was a definite shift in energy on the attention that I would get from people.

Charlotte Cole-Hossain talks about her learning development from a novice cyclist to becoming a youth cycling champion.

I was an under-12 cyclist racing with and against all of the boys. Boys and girls were mixed in altogether for the race. I raced with the same people the year before. They were obviously quite a lot better than me. But in this race, it was the first race back after winter. I'd been doing different training and everything. I'd been doing a lot of cyclo-cross training. I stayed in the front group and I was dropping people who had normally been dropping me in the past. I finished really high up in the top 10 with a group of boys and that was the race after which I thought: 'I could be really good.' You know, these were serious boys, who have been training really hard and properly, whilst I was still kind of doing it just for fun and I managed to stay in there with them.

I started doing quite well that year. I got more and more racing experience. Again, I was racing against the boys and most of them were a year older than me. Those races were all on the track. In terms of road, that same year I placed second in the national circuit championships. Charlotte Broughton won, she had been in the national series and was placing in the top three with the boys throughout. She was like a legend in our days. She was a really fantastic cyclist. So coming second in the national championships was like a win for me.

I was an under-12 in 2011 when I won the national circuit race championships in Bradford, Yorkshire. It had a big hill in it, so for us 12-year-olds it was quite a hard race. I won it by about a tyre's width from my biggest rival at the time, Jessica

Roberts. For the last two years, before that event, we'd been on each other's heels. But I managed to win the sprint by the tiniest bit. After we had finished, I thought that I hadn't won. I was so angry. It wasn't until the podium presentation that it was confirmed that I had in fact won the race. It was very nerve wracking, but eventually a sense of relief. It was the big win for me. I didn't fully expect it, but I was so relieved and so happy, because it was a tough race, a tough course.

For David Clarke, winning was the only option.

Winning the junior Tour of Wales in 1998 when I was 18-years-old was a big achievement for me. I always thought I was going to win it. I could always climb really well. I knew it was hilly. But in my head, I was always going to win it.

Germain Burton talks about topping the field in some of his early hill-climb time trial racing experiences.

My first race was when I was 13 years old, in 2008. It was a hill climb time trial run by the Bec Cycling Club, from Tooting Bec in London. The organiser was Gary Beckett and I'd known him for a long time. His wife was a receptionist at my secondary school and his son was in the school year above mine.

Anyway, that was the first race. It always falls on the second Sunday of October. It was pretty much a local race. My dad helped me with how to train and how to do well in that event. Well, without having any experience of doing time trials, I won the juvenile rider prize and the junior prize that was for riders up to the age of 18. I did quite well, and I was happy. It was a nice way to start things.

It's a race that I have been back to a few times since. In 2010 I managed to win the race and I did it again in 2011. It was quite nice for me, a schoolkid, because the incentive for quite a lot of professional riders travelling from up and down the country was to take home the £1,000 first prize. It was probably quite annoying for some of those riders who had driven down from way up to get beaten by a local kid, snapping up the first prize.

Of course, when I went into school after that, my mates couldn't believe it. It was like: 'What? You earned that much money for less than two minutes' work!'

Russell Williams gives the story of his first national championship win in 1976.

I was 15 years old and one among a group of 15-year-olds. I'd been training regularly for two years down at the track and the coaches were saying: 'Russell, you're going really well. Maybe you should go to the national championships.' Of course, I didn't know what this was all about. They said: 'Yes. It's being held up at Leicester.'

So I went home and spoke with my mum and dad and I said: 'Mum, Dad, the coaches think I should go to the national championships. They think I am good enough to get a medal.'

My dad said to me: 'OK. I am going to take two days off work and I am going to take you up to Leicester. I'm taking you up there.' My dad had a 3.5 litre Rover. He worked as a diesel fitter. So he had to take all tools out of the car to give space for my bike.

We went off to this race, and then halfway up the M1, my dad pulled into the service station and he said: 'OK. We have got to make sure that we get a real good lunch.' So we had this real big lunch, and then when we got to Leicester he had booked us into this bed and breakfast. I was just over the moon, this was me and my dad on this adventure.

So, the next day we went to the track. Things went really well at the championships and I won the national championships. I remember being on the rostrum, looking down, and my dad was smiling. He was really happy. I remember thinking at the time: 'You know what? Maybe I can make it in cycling.' My dream became to make to the Olympics, to go to the world championships.

***

I completed my university studies and graduated, complete with a student debt. I needed to sell things off to be able to eat and to pay my rent. This included my DynaTech time trial bike. Maybe I was trying shift away from racing as well. It was a passion, but at the same time I didn't have a car to get to races I wanted to do. I was always relying on others to get me around. Otherwise, I had to travel to races by train to and from London to Surrey or Sussex.

It was a man called Jim Burrow of the Redmon – one of the old boys with a walrus moustache – who found out I'd sold my bike. He presented me with an old steel framed road racing bike with gear levers on the downtube. It was "to keep me going", he said. I didn't turn it down.

I continued to use that bike for my courier work around London during the spring and summer months of 1999, again clocking up lots of miles on a daily basis. But I missed out defending my club championship time trial title. I no longer had the bike that I needed for that.

I was told that the club hill climb championships would be held at Ranmore Common in October. I hadn't raced hill climb events before but was told that fixed wheel bikes were often used, and the club had a fixed wheel bike, so I arranged to borrow it. I practised on it around Wandsworth Park. It seemed fine. I decided that I would take the train to Westhumble in Dorking to practise on the hill. I knew the hill but didn't know I needed to have brakes on a track bike. I thought I would be able to stop it with my legs in a similar way to what I was doing in the park, where I crashed myself in bushes and trees to stop myself from having a terrible accident.

Eventually I learned to ride the bike with a brake and started to use this for training on the road. It all made sense now. I went on to win the hill climb at Ranmore.

In my head the year 2000 was to be my last year of racing. I took a job as a part-time classroom assistant at a primary school in Tulse Hill. I bought myself a BMX and used that to ride into school. The kids loved seeing me on it. The teachers didn't. I used that bike for training and would often ride flat out, without being able to sit down given the low seat, for four laps around Richmond Park. It did my legs well. In the spring I took out a road racing licence for the first time. I used the bike Jim gave me for some racing at the Hillingdon Circuit. When I won my first race, I just broke away from the group early on and time trialled it for 10 laps alone to the chequered flag. I won a few more races that season, and I moved quickly from category 4 to 2.

My final event that year was a 60-mile race on a rolling course in Rusper, West Sussex, held by the Surrey League. I hitched a lift out there from Mick, as Redmon were also running a time trial in the same area that morning. The roads were twisty and the race went by quickly. I had made it my habit in road races to be at the front on the penultimate lap so as rehearse where I would be taking my sprint from. The last lap came and I had seen Mick hanging around by the finish line. He did say that he might come over to watch, maybe even give me a lift back to London.

The bunch seemed to be together. We swooped around the corner and began to climb the hill to the finish. I decided to make a move to get closer to the front. I jumped up and pulled – but also accidentally unclipped out of my pedal. For some reason I just could not get my shoe clipped back in, as almost every rider behind me passed by. I slipped to the back.

I got the shoe in and sprinted, passing as many riders as I could, until it was me and a couple of others left at the front. I won the sprint. I wasn't aware of any riders ahead but expected that there were some.

I came back down the road. "How many people were in front of me?" I asked Mick.

"There was no one," he said. "You won it!"

CHAPTER 5
I JUST BEAT THE REST OF THEM OUT OF SIGHT

Big sponsors lined up to support riders ahead of the 1984 Olympics and this warm-up at the Los Angeles Olympic Velodrome attracted a huge crowd. Silver medallist at the Games later that year, Nelson Vails, stands for the national anthem. Gold medallist Mark Gorski is on his right

The White Hope sprinters competition was a cycling event held annually as part of the world-renowned Good Friday International Track Cycling Meeting at Herne Hill. It no longer takes this name, but an Eastertime sprint competition continues for aspirant amateurs, although now held at the London Olympic Velodrome. The racial connotation of 'White Hope' emanates from the early 1900s, when the first ever recognised black world heavyweight boxing champion, Jack Johnson, appeared to be invincible. The term 'Great White Hope' was applied to any white challenger who took him on. It also applied to those who challenged Major Taylor, particularly after he became a double world champion in 1899. One upcoming 'White Hope' and a rival of Taylor's was Eddie Kramer and their match sprint race of 30 June 1900 was touted 'as the great white hope versus the black world champion!' Nevertheless that day Taylor beat Kramer.

When it comes to the White Hope Sprint, the name became ironic.
Russell Williams first rode the event in 1976.

I wasn't really a 'pure sprinter', but it was man on man. I remember I was up against a big German. I don't know whether he was the Olympic champion or something. But, thinking back, I am sure that when we were playing around on the first lap he pulled his foot out, and I should have gone then. No hesitation. Just gone.

But I thought, with him being Olympic champion or whatever he was, the correct thing to do was to wait, be a gentleman, whilst he was up the top of the track putting in his foot back in. I remember it. I might have had the edge of starting the race behind him. The Herne Hill track is not that steep, but I should have just taken off, and I would have been in the next round.

But anyway, it was a couple of years later in 1978 when I won the competition. Which was big because at that time it was the big race for up-and-coming sprinters all around Great Britain, and because it was on my home track as well.

The attitude necessary to dominate opponents and secure victory after victory can help create an immunity to racial prejudice directed at the black cyclist. Major Taylor set an extremely high standard for any competitive black racing cyclist to follow in this regard; a tenacity and a resilience to explicit racial gamesmanship, including physical violence. His career record in the USA and across the world suggests that although racism was explicit and direct in aiming to kill his force he, like Vails, was winning and this was hurting the pride of his opponents much more than they could hurt his.

Russell Williams at the velodrome, Saffron Lane
Sports Centre, Leicester in 1987

IT WAS BIG BECAUSE AT THAT TIME IT WAS THE BIG RACE FOR UP-AND-COMING SPRINTERS ALL AROUND GREAT BRITAIN AND BECAUSE IT WAS ON MY HOME TRACK AS WELL

RUSSELL WILLIAMS

93

Nobody that I had met in cycling had ever mentioned Major Taylor to me, his life, and his racing career. Maybe those people I knew did not know about him? Maybe it was because he was American? Maybe it was because he was black? Maybe, but at the same time nobody had really told me about Maurice Burton's dominance on the track either and he was a black man from South London, his shop just a few miles from where I lived. I had read about Russell Williams' victories and his dominance at Herne Hill and Crystal Palace, and I did catch glimpses and news about Mark McKay in *Cycling Weekly*, particularly when he raced for Team Ambrosia and with Team Harrods. But I wasn't aware that he was able to dominate the elite road men in the hills and beat them all on his day.

Young black British and African American cyclists in their ascendency were all able to dominate the racing proceedings at national level. Russell Williams reflects on his 1976 racing season including a hat trick of national championship victories.

I won my first national title at the age of 15. In fact, I did the double in that championships at Leicester, taking the junior sprint title and the 2km junior pursuit title. I was training hard by that age and was well into it by then.

Later in that year, I won the national junior road race. I broke away from the field to catch the break. They were about one minute ahead, and then when I caught the leading break, I broke away from that group to win solo. It was a great day. I just loved the taste of victory.

Arguably one of the best British junior road and track riders of his generation, Russell was rightly rewarded with selection to represent Great Britain at the world junior men's road racing championships.

Rahsaan Bahati shares a story about his dominant winning streak as junior road racer. And, just like his first national track championship win, adversity was the fuel behind his repeated triumphs.

We had a stage race which was like the Tour de l'Avenir. It was called the Best of the West, a six-day junior stage race in the North West of the USA.

As a junior rider, I always wanted to go to this race. My parents didn't have a lot of money. But my coaches were saying: "Look, you gotta try to get your son to this race." So my dad wanted to try to figure this out. We didn't have a car with bike racks. So he rented out a hauler van. It took us forever to get there. The van had a lot of mechanical issues.

On the very first stage, the race is coming out of the mountain and I become confident about the race as it is going to come down to a sprint finish. But I crashed and I snapped my collarbone.

It's the first time I have ever crashed in a race. The first time I have broken a bone in my body. I am out of the race on the very first day.

I just remember being so sad that my dad had used all of the resources that he could come up with to get me there, and now I can't participate. A lot of people thought I was crying because of my injury. But I was just so sad for the sacrifice that my dad had made.

But there was a blessing that came out of this. We finally got home, and I got hold of a turbo trainer, and I rode on it every day for an hour with my arm in a sling. When I was able to ride my bike three weeks later, I went up to Oakland, California to stay with a friend and trained with him. On my very first race back, it was 4 July, I got fourth or fifth in the pro race. I was just 16 years old. From that point forward, I won 19 races in a row. I went on a tear.

Clocking up that sort of winning streak year after year would become Bahati's signature approach.

From the end of 2006 to the end of 2010, people would show up on the line next to me knowing that they were going for second place. I took everything I could get then because I knew that another generation was coming up. I would get slower, not be the same. I had about three to three-and-a-half years as the dominant force.

I talk to people now who I used to race against and they tell me stories like: 'Ah man! Bahati's here, what are we going to do to get second?' I had no idea that they were thinking like that. But I had the confidence in myself to know that I could win. When you have that confidence, sometimes it is hard to let it go.

That sort of realisation of confidence and strength is also reflected in the accounts of Justin Williams. He speaks about his early days of race 'schooling' which would develop his strategic and ruthless capabilities to win.

I would win the junior races in the morning and then race the Category 3 races with my dad. He would lead me out for wins.

The reason I was so dominant was because I had figured out the racing. I was 16, and I think I won 90% of my Category 3 races. I won around 25 or 26 races with the Major Motion team.

The Category 3 riders were either retired pros, or masters who used to be pros. Later on in the afternoon, I would jump in the pro races, just to see what I could do. It was school for me. I would get top 20, even top 10. I actually got kicked out of the Category 3 races because I was a junior winning them.

Some riders recall specific victories as being a turning point. Sometimes the victory is at a national event, others at a big event against other talented cyclists. Christian Lyte remembers both – firstly through his under-16 British national match sprint championship and then in beating riders already recruited to the national talent pool.

It was the first big race that projected me. I won sprint gold. That was in Newport, Wales in 2005. But, before that, I also used to compete in the Revolutions series races in 2003 and 2004. There was a competition for future stars. I won the scratch race. I also won the elimination race, and a few of the guys who were in that race were already on the British Cycling Talent Team. Most people were racing on those yellow Corima carbon racing bikes. But I was racing on a steel framed bike and winning.

Maurice Burton had a similar experience of competing with lesser equipment. But once that gap had been addressed, his first national title came with supreme confidence.

Maurice Burton as a 22-year-old professional in Belgium in 1978

I'd never ridden on a steep track before. I was on a Greater London Council hire bicycle, and I ended up in fourth place in 1972.

Anyway, I went again [the next year]. Youngs Cycles of Lee High Road in Lewisham gave me a proper track bike. I went up there on the train. I slept the night on the floor in the table tennis room. The next day, I just beat the rest of them out of sight and I won the British championships for the junior sprint competition.

Germain Burton's affirmation came when, aged 15, he beat the British elite road racing champion on the way to winning the prestigious Bec Hill Climb.

I think that is what people remember me for the most. There were some top

Charlotte Cole-Hossain at the 2015
British Youth Championships points
race held in Manchester, a race she
would win as a junior in 2016

domestic professional riders there like Kristian House. He was the British road race champion in 2009. It was just fun at the time. I was still at school. I trained really hard for it. I enjoyed racing.

Cycling Weekly wrote about it. They were talking about me as the 'local boy' winning big. There were so many people out there on that day. People still talk to me about it.

The doubt going into a championship race is erased by the magic that comes from belief, as <u>Charlotte Cole-Hossain</u> testifies.

I won the British points race championships for junior women in 2016 as a first year rider. I felt very much like the underdog at the beginning of this race. But I just attacked.

I guess I had become known for attacking whenever I got the chance. I went off the front. I think the other riders kind of hesitated a bit in the chase. But I managed to get maybe half a lap as a gap, and I could see that no-one wanted to commit too much. It was early in the race. I was holding the bunch. I got the first set of five points. I stayed away for another six or seven laps and I started to see the back of the bunch. I thought: 'This is really tempting. I would love to get that lap.' I thought: 'Hold back! Just hold back! Just get the next five points, and then see if you can close them down.'

I was the entire time looking at the leaderboard. I stayed back. I got the five points and managed to stay on as well. I thought: 'This is crazy!' because I never dreamt that I'd medal and I was in the top spot with two sprints to go.

For BMX riders, feeling the momentum of excellence gives that greater sense of belief. <u>Tre Whyte</u> speaks of his progression from grassroots excellence as a youth rider to dominance at national level including championship race wins.

When I was 11 years old, I finished in second place at three or four of the BMX national series races. I also finished in second place at the BMX national championships in 2005. I think my breakthrough race was when I was 15 years old and I became the British BMX champion in 2009. From that moment onwards, I kept on excelling. I was racing up a level against the junior riders. I was a 15-year-old racing against riders who were aged 17 or 18. I won national series events. I won the British BMX championships in 2015. Again, in the 2016 championships, I won that race.

Tre's contemporary <u>Quillan Isidore</u> gives the story of his dominance in the 2012 season where he was virtually unbeatable on the national scene, and ultimately elevated himself further to become the BMX world champion.

Practice went perfect and I felt super confident. I won all my heats and 1/8th final before I had a four-hour break before the main events started. In two out of the four rounds I had to work my way through the pack to finish first which taught me a few vital areas to keep in mind before the quarters, semi and final.

[As the session went on] the stands filled with spectators. I was nervous but managed to get out good and lead out the quarter final. The semi-final was probably my best lap of the day. I got out great and didn't make a single mistake. I was buzzing – I bounced with excitement over the finish line making my first world championship final.

The final was something else. The roar from the crowd blew me away. Before the race I was very chilled speaking to reigning champion, Sean Gaian from the USA, to the world number two, Chris Christensen from Denmark. We were having a laugh and enjoying the moment. But when it was time to focus I was so in the zone.

Boom: gate drops and I got a great gate, by far my fastest first straight of the day and holeshotted [reached the first corner in the lead]. I heard the crowd roar but kept focus and kept the lead into the second corner without a mistake and was going super-fast creating a big lead.

Going down the third straight I made a mistake and couldn't do the line I was doing all day which was the faster one. This is when it popped into my head that I'm actually winning the world championship final. I did it. I won the world championships in my home country! I bounced across the line and chucked my bike and soaked up the roar from the crowd.

Quillan and Tre stand on the shoulders of black British BMX champions such as Charlie Reynolds. He gives an account of his confidence to dominate race proceedings and to put money where his mouth was for the big races.

My second Champion of Champions title race at Olympia in London was my breakthrough race. I was on fire. I think that I actually won the race by an entire straight.

1985 was a dominant year for me. I cleaned up. I was Champion of Champions and 24-inch Cruiser champion.

The Champion of Champions racing for me is like the FA Cup. It is the best of the best riders from all regions coming together [at the end of the season].

Riders [like me] couldn't afford to get to every single national event, so couldn't get the number one plate. But I was always champion of champions regardless.

Some of those other riders may have gone to all of the national events and trumped up the points because their parents had got them there. But on the big day, at the Champion of Champions weekend, don't bother about the points that you have been collating, this day you are getting roasted by me.

CHAPTER 6 BOYCOTT OF THE BLACK PRESENCE

Wayne Llewellyn racing for Ammaco Mongoose pro BMX team in 1984

WHEN I WAS YOUNGER, I NEVER REALLY SAW MYSELF AS BLACK OR WHITE. I JUST SAW MYSELF AS ME. BUT I WAS CALLED 'GOLLYWOG' AND WHATEVER ELSE, THAT JUST FLEW OVER MY HEAD

WAYNE LLEWELLYN

BMX athletes such as Charlie Reynolds, Wayne Llewellyn and Luli Adeyemo were at the centre of a thriving cycling scene in the 1980s in which black athletic excellence was fully on show. Perhaps the race that best tells the story of this period is the 1986 professional BMX World Championships. Held in Slough in the south east of England, the final was contested by eight riders – five of whom were black, among them the winner and runner-up. Meanwhile an association of white British professional riders chose to boycott races at the event due to a black rider Gary Llewellyn (older brother of Wayne) being permitted to race by the International BMX Federation. British BMX was booming by the mid-80s, gaining national attention. In 1985, the UK BMX Schweppes Grand Prix season opener at Hounslow attracted over 1,000 entries, a record for a UK-based BMX race at the time.

Races at that national event would occur over just one day, from midday through to the evening, and saw winning performances from brothers Gary and Wayne Llewellyn and from Charlie Reynolds. All came from South London. Over in the west of the capital, quality riders came from the Westway BMX club, including the charismatic six-foot-four-inches Winston Wright and other talented racers such as Errol Mclean and Shaun Bailey, today better known as a Conservative politician who stood for London mayor in 2021.

But black athlete talent and excellence in BMX during the 1980s was not confined to London. Luli Adeyemo was from Newark in the East Midlands, and the Birmingham Wheels BMX club featured strong riders such as Trevor Robinson and his cousin Pat.

Some of these riders found their profiles further boosted by featuring on *Kellogg's BMX Track Wars*, a popular weekly TV show. Of them, most attention was perhaps generated by the Llewellyn brothers – known for their ruthless race-winning talents – and by Charlie Reynolds, through his regular victories.

Charlie Reynolds reflects on knowing he was set to do something special in sport despite the hostilities he faced as a teenager.

I remember, at school, my teacher said to me: 'You're not going to amount to anything.' But I did my talking physically through sport. I was a pure athlete. All the others were smoking joints. I didn't touch anything. I didn't even drink Pepsi Cola! Back in those days of living in the south of London, in Stockwell, it was difficult. I remember being stopped by the police and them just taking my bike for no reason. I think it was because I was a black man. Eventually, they had to give it back. It belonged to the shop that I was sponsored by.

The development of BMX and skateboarding parks in areas such as Stockwell and Romford allowed riders including Reynolds and the Llewellyns to cross paths and to become close friends. Wayne Llewellyn also recounts the support given by parents of BMX-loving children and fellow racers.

We should all be thankful to Sue and Malcolm Jarvis [who started the Ammaco Mongoose team]. Also, a guy called Ken Walkling. He was from Lewisham. He had a fruit and veg stall. I don't know if it was all that very profitable, but out of his own pocket, he built us a BMX track. For me, my brother, his two, and Charlie. He done wonders for us, that man. He never had a bike or anything. He just wanted the best for young people.

The BMX and skateboarding parks enabled development of raw skill and talent, creating future world beaters and stunt innovators, as Charlie recounts.

I was the big influence for skatepark and street BMX. People would follow me. They used to say: 'Charlie's doing this and doing that over at the park.' I was street jumping on to car bonnets, and off them again. I always tried the un-triable; the un-thinkable. They'd say: 'Don't jump that!' But I wouldn't hear that. I'd always launch myself across things before anyone else did.

It was cool to be at the skateparks, and street riding with Gary and Wayne.

I know it sounds terrible, but we never ever trained. We didn't need to. We rode the streets. We 'spun out' on the streets. That gave us that speed and power on the track. It was from the streets that we got our straight-line power. We were naturals. Everyone else was going to gate practice. I admit I wasn't the best starter, but my second pedal was the one that killed off others in my races, and if I did have a good start, I'd wipe the floor with everyone.

After one year of racing and introducing themselves to the BMX world, the dominance of this generation of young, talented black riders began. Wayne and his brother Gary attracted sponsorship from Britain's number one BMX team Ammaco Mongoose. Wayne describes these beginnings.

We used to race over at Eastway and at Buckmore Park. In my first year I must have raced about nine times. I won seven of those races. I was the national number nine rider. The following year I was national number one. Then Mongoose sponsored me. My brother Gary was signed to the Ammaco Mongoose BMX team for three years. I was on the team for four years.

Up until I finished, I was always number one in Britain in my age category. It was as though I could ride in BMX as if I were born to do it. At many regional and national races, I used to ride up an age group, I was that quick.

There was one year where I won 32 out of 34 races. In one of them, I came last because I had fallen off the bike. In the other one, I came second because I sat down and looked to my left – I was about to win, and a rider overtook me on the right.

Gary Llewellyn racing in Wigan 1985 over the infamous jump named 'King Kong' by the racers

We would get picked up and dropped off by Ammaco Mongoose to go to races whether they were in Bromley, Birmingham, Scotland, wherever. We went all over Europe.

Gary was the British champion for few years running. He didn't win the Europeans or the Worlds because he fell off the bike in races. But he was a strong rider. When the American guys like Tommy Brackens used to come over, Gary would often beat them. He would beat everyone in England: Andy Ruffell; Pete Middleton, Craig Schofield, Martin Joyce, Jamie Vince.

If BMX were an Olympic sport back in those days, we'd definitely have been racing for Great Britain. We were that good.

Charlie's path to the top began with Brixton BMX Club under the mentorship of Ken Floyd. He attracted the attention of Edwardes Cycles Racing Team in Camberwell and began racing for them. <u>Charlie</u> shares some insights about his rise to the national attention of the BMX world.

I started getting involved in races and then, before you know it, I was beating the British number one rider. In fact, the second time I saw him, I beat him! That's how it was.

A year later, I remember walking into a newsagents and being shocked to see me on the front cover of not one but three BMX magazines. I was in the national *Observer* magazine as the fastest 'rising star' on the British BMX circuit. I ran out the shop and ran home and shouted: 'Mum! I'm famous!'

I remember how my carers from the children's home came rushing down from Gloucestershire to where I worked at

Edwardes Cycles in London. They were so excited about it. They were saying:

'Charlie! You've made it, you're famous!' My career as a racer took off.

Charlie Reynolds interviewed after landing another trademark '360' jump at the 1990 IBMXF World Championships in France

All of this excitement was coupled with frustration at not being able to attract a full factory sponsorship deal, despite regularly beating the best of his peers, who had been granted such deals.

Winning my number one plate as British cruiser champion in 1985 at Wigan was a great day. But as time went on, I also remember that somebody once wrote in a magazine: 'Charlie Reynolds is Number 1. How comes he doesn't have a full factory sponsor? Something is wrong.' I did not think too much about that at the time. I had so much merchandise being thrown at me from the USA. I just never really had it before in life that people would continually be giving me things.

But I came to realise that it was the co-sponsors of the shop that I rode for that were supplying the merchandise. I felt like none of the big major teams were willing or able to sign me. I also noticed that the white riders behind me, ranked at number two, three, four and five in the country, were 'creaming' it. They were driving big company cars and looking the part. I just didn't know the scale of money that was being offered from the big sponsors like Raleigh.

The Ammaco Mongoose team was arguably the top British BMX team of the era, filled with the British number one riders in their age categories. Wayne and Gary were part of that clique. Gary was developing his palmares as a multiple national champion, whilst Wayne was not only continuing to build on his multiple national championships but also became the first British rider to win a hattrick of European BMX titles in 1982, 1983 and in 1984. The following year, he was also crowned a world champion.

The World Championships race win, I remember it was severely downhill. It was a really fast race. I planned it. I watched them all, then pounced. I won it on the last berm. I went on the inside and banged the other guy out a bit and won it there. I got a trophy. I got myself in the magazines. But the main thing you get is a boost to your self-esteem in what you are and what you have done.

But Wayne too was beginning to see some differences in the value ascribed to him compared to that of white riders with fewer titles.

Ammaco Mongoose signed all of the number one riders. At that time, I was one of the top and respected racers.

From the age of 14 to 16, I used to get £1,000 a month sponsorship money. I used to think that was a lot of money.

Tommy Brackens, Anthony Sewell and Turnell Henry at the Corona, California, 1981

I think I was on the TV every other week. Another rider in my team, a white guy, got so much more money than I did. It's strange. He wasn't even a world champion. We used to do demonstration rides together. I read in a national newspaper about how much he was getting compared to me. He was getting £28k a year for the same work and time as me. I went nuts about it.

Charlie had a similar experience.

I knew that there was discrimination going on. Back in the days of 1984 to 1985 there was a large contingency of black BMX riders. But it took some time before Nicky Matthews became the first black British guy that I saw in a magazine.

I remember when the children's TV programme *John Craven's Newsround* came to film at an event. I'd won the race. I was showcasing, doing all sorts of stunts in the air and everything for them. But I don't think one black person was the main feature in the film that went out. You know, sometimes we used to go to the hotels the night before races and they'd ask the black riders to pay in advance but not the white riders.

Ultimately Charlie would turn his attention to stunts over racing – a reaction to the continuing lack of full factory sponsorship that he so desired.

I wasn't looked after as a rider. That is the reason why I was not 100% committed. I thought to myself: 'Why the hell was I trying to make it as a BMX rider?' I had no team bus. No funding.

So I left the sport for a while. I came back to BMX in 1989 and started focusing on my stunts, because I knew the impact that was having on the sport. I reinvented myself. People enjoyed the crashing and the tension between getting it wrong and getting it right the next time. Magazines couldn't close their eyes to this. I was on the front cover of three French magazines following my groundbreaking 720 jumps at the World Championships in 1991.

Charlie even had a bicycle manufactured and named after him, perhaps a first for a black BMX cyclist. But he still had reason to feel he was not being fully cared for and not benefiting from his own success.

I was given the run of the floor in the factory. I had a signature bike made. But when thinking about it, I felt that my name and popularity were being used to help the sales of the bikes with not much money coming out of it for me. Although I was a pioneer in being one of first black professional riders to have a signature bike named after him, I made no money.

**

British BMX during the mid-1980s generated such an energy that it became the centre of attention of the sport. All of this meant that foreign riders, including from the USA, were attracted to the scene. African American professionals such as Antony Sewell and Tommy Brackens began to come to stay in Britain to compete in races.

For <u>Charlie</u>, being in the presence of these riders offered a new perspective on what black British athletes could – or more accurately might have – become.

I think that I would have had more influence and desire to build my professional career if I had known more about these guys and what they were doing in the sport before they came over here to race. In the UK magazines I only really saw pictures and read about the domestic white champions of the sport. I didn't know about these black BMX champions from the USA who were the best in the world. Antony Sewell was the world champion in 1978. I did not know about this.

They would have been our role models and inspired us black British riders to have done more. I didn't know about Antony Sewell or Jarrett Justice. It only took hold when Tommy Brackens won the Worlds.

That was at the fateful 1986 championships in Slough, when the black athlete presence in the men's professional final was greater than white riders, an extreme rarity in the history of competitive cycling.

But it was an occurrence which came about in controversial circumstances. Many of the English professional riders were demanding more financial rewards from the sport, and so formed their own body to begin to govern themselves. It was this riders' association that took action to prevent Gary from racing, as Charlie recounts.

Believe it or not, the English team boycotted the 1986 World Championships in Slough because Gary was able to race up a category. Gary and Wayne were huge physical athletes for their ages, and I can remember when Gary had been to Slough before and gave them all a roasting. All the people winning titles in Europe and all over, when they came back, they were getting beaten in races by Wayne, and Gary was burning up everyone. He just didn't take it seriously. They also didn't realise he was a young man with mental health issues.

He wasn't supported with this.

Anyway, the UK BMX rider association managed to have Gary barred from racing on the UK BMX scene, under their accusations of rider misconduct or something. But the International BMX Federation was running the event. They let Gary take part. The UK BMX pro riders had egg on their faces from this, you know, those who had been beaten so many times by the up-and-coming riders like Gary.

They knew that Gary was quick, and they weren't happy about him racing up. So they didn't race in it.

But I think that there was another reason behind it. There were some riders who weren't down with the black presence in the sport. You just know these kinds of guys by their attitudes. Anyway, Gary was able to get in as an independent racer.

I got toasted in that race, because me and Gary came from a nightclub the night before. We didn't think we were racing because of the ban and the boycott. From the entire grid there were five black men in that final: me and Gary from Britain; with Shawn Texas, Tommy Brackens and Antony Sewell from the USA. Tommy became the world champion that day. I came sixth, and Gary placed seventh. We just weren't on it.

Anthony Sewell leads the rest through a berm at the Cook Classic in 1980. Anthony became number one in 1980 for both the National Bicycle Association (NBA) and the National Bicycle League (NBL). He also became the first rider to pull a 'no-hander' jump

Tommy Brackens was not the only black BMX athlete to become a world champion on that day in Slough. Luli Adeyemo was the first black British female BMX champion, yet gained little attention during her career. <u>Charlie</u> gives his perspective on just why that was.

Luli didn't even end up in the magazines, and this is extraordinary given her wins. I don't know if it was because she was quite dark skinned. I mean Sarah Jane Nichols and Karen Murphy were white British girls. They were both very talented, and always in the magazines. But in all the magazines that I have got from back in the day, Luli is not in any of them.

<u>Luli Adeyemo's</u> story is extraordinary. Adopted as a baby by white British parents, she grew up in a white-dominant neighbourhood in Newark in the Midlands. When a new BMX track was built close to where she lived, one day she decided to visit it – even though she didn't know how to ride a bicycle.

A friend offered to sell her a BMX for £50 but Luli's mother refused to pay for it, reasoning it would soon be gathering dust; another fleeting teenage interest. So Luli saved up the money herself, bought the bike, and began learning to ride it at the BMX track.

I wasn't like a duck taking to water at first, but after a few months, something just clicked in my mind, and I could ride so fast.

<u>Luli</u> practised nearly every day, and eventually joined her local club. She racked up decent placings at races across the country and was offered an opportunity to race at the 1986 World Championships.

I was totally overwhelmed and so incredibly excited. It was my first international event so I hadn't seen anything of that magnitude. I only had started competing nationally that year so hadn't qualified via the usual channels – I'd been invited to compete as a wild card.

Nobody, including me, really expected me to get through the motos – let alone make it to the finals. There's something beautiful about being the underdog, absolutely zero pressure and just being grateful to be at the start gate with some of the greats of the sport. Back then the Dutch were the ones to beat, quick out the gate and strong.

I started off slowly getting the minor positions in the motos, but in the semis I made my mark, putting me in a good position to be competitive in the final. But nobody thought I'd actually win. Jumping the doubles on the third straight gave me a significant advantage that I was able to hold onto to keep the lead. My strengths were I was quick out of the gate and I could jump.

For Luli, the British BMX scene of the 1980s allowed her to socialise with the sort of young black peers she'd rarely encountered previously due to her adoption and strongly white neighbourhood.

I remember the minibuses arriving at events with music blasting out, the vibes. I wasn't really sponsored. My coach down at the local BMX track was my friend's dad, Darryl Pointing, who had zero coaching, sporting, or cycling background. I was taken under the wing of Winston Wright [another black rider]. He was great, like a big brother to me.

I asked Luli whether she saw anybody with her identity on the scene during the 1980s:

"Absolutely none – I was it!"

Today Luli lives in Australia and the story of her sporting career is almost forgotten despite being extraordinary – a young and enthusiastic black British girl who one year learnt to ride a BMX, grabbed the opportunity of a wildcard at the World Championships, and became a world champion at first time of asking.

***

The British BMX scene of the 1980s began to cool when Ammaco Mongoose pulled away. Although Raleigh bikes aimed to maintain the energy, the huge attention that BMX had once commanded lessened. Wayne Llewellyn had a particularly tough time during this period.

I was 16 when Ammaco Mongoose folded, BMX folded and that was it. My dad died. I was homeless for a few weeks. I was put in a bedsit. My brother was sectioned. My life went into total darkness.

There is a fearlessness in BMX racing which requires a warrior mindset. Wayne Llewellyn had that and it is tough to stop a champion, even one who has experienced such hard times. He moved from BMX to professional boxing, winning over 40 bouts as a heavyweight fighter. Today he works through his own company that brings the discipline of boxing into schools, serving as a role model for children.

***

Peckham BMX, a club run by former racer Michael Pusey, is an example of how that 1980s scene has evolved. Michael has mentored some of Britain's best black BMX riders in recent years: Tre Whyte, Kye Whyte and Quillan Isidore among them.

There are clubs all across Britain, but it seems BMX remains most
closely associated with inner-city street and urban subculture.
Perhaps that's why it seems to be the only form of competitive cycling
that young black people have the chance to excel in? Images of black
riders promote BMX at the National Cycling Centre in Manchester,
whilst white faces are presented as the figureheads of road racing,
track cycling, mountain biking – a statement of ethnic categorisation
in cycling.

Interestingly, Sir Chris Hoy – Britain's best Olympian – began his
racing career as a BMX rider, and was later afforded the opportunity
to switch to track sprinting. This experiment also worked successfully
with the black BMX rider Shanaze Reade. However, the opportunity
to represent Great Britain has never been afforded to world-
championship-winning black male BMX riders; they've never had
the chance to test whether their talents are transferable to track
sprinting. BMX is all about power, sprinting, strength. Could Tre and
Kye Whyte, and Quillan Isidore, have been slotted in alongside the
likes of Chris Hoy and Jason Kenny on the national track sprint team?
And how would the likes of Wayne and Gary Llewellyn, Charlie
Reynolds or Luli Adeyamo have fared on the velodrome boards?

CHAPTER 7 THE DARK DESTROYER

Justin Williams, US champion and
Red Bull-sponsored athlete in 2021

I FELT SOME OF THE DECISIONS WERE BECAUSE OF ME BEING A BLACK KID. I HAVE DEALT WITH RACIST PEOPLE... BUT I WAS A KID AND I WAS ROBBED OF TWO NATIONAL TITLES

JUSTIN WILLIAMS

I'd never stopped riding my bike, never stopped being addicted to cycling. But racing? That I'd stopped, as it had become a struggle to get to races while dependent on public transport or a friendly lift. The break lasted five years in all but came to an end when I finally acquired a car and, with it, the means to travel to races under my own steam; the ability to turn up at any starting line in the country. I joined Agiskoviner cycling team. It brought together some of the best London- and South East-based category 1 and 2 riders, all of them white. But I wasn't in fact the only black rider on the squad. Ashley Lambert and I raced together in a couple of circuit races. His presence was short lived, however. After one season of racing, he left England and returned to his home in Zimbabwe. The Agiskoviner cycling team had big ambitions. The aim was to win national championships.

It was a level of racing I hadn't ever thought about before. But the ambitious message appealed to me.

One of my first events in Agiskoviner team colours was an early season criterium. I had been strong all day, having already been part of a four-man break that had been pulled back. With a few laps to go, I decided to jump again. Some of my team-mates were spectators at the race and saw my attack. They shouted out as I rode by them.

I knew I was up for winning this one and so I decided to try to solo for the last lap. It didn't work. I got swallowed up with about a kilometre to go and eventually rolled in at the back.

Afterwards I passed my team-mates who'd been watching the race. "Great ride, Marlon!" said one.

"The dark destroyer!" another called out.

The veil was dropped; racially conditioned thoughts revealed. Here was a white man using a racial reference (the ring name of the British boxer Nigel Benn) to describe my efforts.

I hadn't expected that from my team-mate. And why should I have done? The hypervisibility of my skin colour brought out this example of racially conditioned thinking. It would never have crossed my mind to racially reference his efforts by borrowing a white boxer's ring name.

It is no secret that white people talk amongst themselves about black people and cycling. In 2009, I came across a discussion on timetrailingforum.co.uk entitled 'Whites only'. The thread opens with the words.

Time trialling has always been a mainly male sport – the figures show it; but throughout my 45 years of involvement with the pastime, it has always been a virtually 100% white sport. Yes, I know we can always quote 'what about so-and-so who used to be in the whatsit wheelers' – but generally, our scene does not appeal to our ethnic brethren, and you very rarely see a rider with anything more than a suntan. Any thoughts as to why?

What followed was a range of ignorant comments based on the pseudo-science of racism and a revealing look at the white gaze that has been cast upon black people in cycling.

Firstly, I wonder if the physiological differences of black and Asian people in comparison with Caucasian has any bearing? Apart from Major Taylor from around 100yrs ago and a handful of black and Asian sprinters (the 84 Olympic Sprint Champ) I can't think of a single world class black or Asian road rider.

Ironically, the year in which this was posted was the year in which Grégory Baugé became world track sprint champion. The ignorant racist assumptions continue.

This situation exists in swimming and is apparently due to average leg length as proportion of total height being longer and thus the smaller torso causes less buoyancy. Perhaps in cycling there's an issue here that causes a lower than the (average) Caucasian power to weight ratio rendering endurance cycling a more difficult sport in which to be competitive with Caucasians.

At last an intervention to the ignorance occurs where a contributor speaks to acknowledge underlying currents of racism embedded in the attitudes of white club riders.

I do believe there are many cultural and societal contributing factors as well as a certain low-level racist undertone amongst many clubmen (in my experience).

Whether this contributor is speaking to the ignorance of the forum that he is part of or not, it is a perspective which relates to the vibe I picked up from my team-mate. It's one that was also experienced by Tim Erwin.

Years ago, when I was racing in Louisiana, an official and her husband were always nice to me. But I remember once after I had just finished a crit as a junior, we were all in this little group chatting and the husband had a Breathe Right strip-type thing that flared his nostrils. I asked him about it and his wife said, without skipping a beat: 'Oh, that gives him his *nigger* nose.' I was 16 I think, and I said: 'What did you say?' She fumbled for her words and said: 'Ah, um, I will buy you a snow cone,' as if that would make everything okay. That was 30 years ago but it is just another example of the things I've personally experienced.

I'd worked my way back to racing with the E12 road riders, taking some nice wins. One was at a stage race held in Sussex. There had been a big crash at 5km to the finish and it was clear the race was going to come down to a sprint. I had got myself into a great position in the end and I took the chequered flag, by a tyre's width.

Another rider, though, thought he'd taken it. There was a polite dispute between the two of us and so we approached one of the race organisers, Glyn Durrant. He confirmed I'd won it. Yes! It was my last event of the season, and a good end to a good year of racing. A local dignitary was around to hand out medals, and there would be a photo opportunity for the local paper.

I was getting ready to go over to the podium. I turned and saw Glyn walking over to my car. I noticed that he had bit of an apologetic tone about him.

"Marlon. The chief commissaire would like to have a word with you."

"Hmm. Why is that?"

"I think he is going to disqualify you."

"What? For what!?"

"I don't know. Go and see him."

"Where is he?"

Glyn pointed to the chief commissaire's car.

***

<u>Maurice Burton</u> also experienced special attention from the commissaires.

The 100km event at Crystal Palace on a Sunday brings back a memory. There was a certain official who was very much in charge of things, a certain Mr Wingrave. I'd already raced in Belgium by this time, and I'd been in a Belgium amateur team. I had these shorts on, and it was showing the sponsor. The letters were going across the shorts. On the start line, Mr Wingrave came across to me and said: 'You won't be able to ride because you have got advertising on your shorts.'

I looked at him, in thought for a brief moment. He looked at me. I then turned the shorts over to make them hide the advertising. I said: 'Is that OK, Mr Wingrave?' I knew he was after me from the beginning. He didn't have much to say after that. He walked away.

I got in the race. I got in the break and got away with a former professional rider called John Clary. This man had ridden in the Tour de France. I won. I won the sprint. I beat John, and John congratulated me. He put his arm on my shoulder and said: 'Well done.'

A few minutes later it was different story because Mr Wingrave decided I didn't win it – I came second, and John won it.

I think there were people watching who were angrier than me on that day. I just looked at it and put it down to experience. I thought: 'If I ever am involved in a race again with Mr Wingrave as the official I better make sure that I win it a bit more than a few inches.'

To do that to a 19-year-old boy. It didn't surprise me. The fact is that a few years before this when Mr Wingrave was in charge of the races that I won at Crystal Palace, he came over to me, and said: 'You won't win any races next year.' It didn't surprise me. I smiled at him.

Maurice also remembers receiving extra special surveillance by officials when he was defending his British Championships 20km title in 1975.

In the final, I was boxed in by some of the guys and I had to push my way out to stand a chance. I got through and possibly still might have won it, even though I was coming at it much later than I wanted. But a guy moved up on me, and his pedal went into my wheel. I crashed heavily on the home straight just before the line. I was on the floor. I didn't get to finish the race.

And do you know, they [the officials] claimed that I pulled a rider. But I didn't, I had leaned on him. I mean, how can you disqualify me when I didn't even finish the race? [It was] for no reason apart from that they wanted to put the boot in. I didn't finish! But they had to make the point by saying: 'You're disqualified!'

The incident and his treatment on that day contributed heavily to Maurice's loss of appetite for racing in his home country. "I was a bit down after those championships," he remembers. "I left England afterwards."

Charlie Reynolds also knows the pain of being deprived of a win by biased commissaires. In 1985, he was well placed to take a number one plate. He only needed to take fourth place to take the title. But one of the race officials just happened to be the team manager of one of his closest rivals.

How can you have his team boss as an official in the same race? The guy who was losing his title came around the corner and smashed me off. I got back on the bike, and still managed to finish fourth. I was truly the double British BMX champion: 24-inch cruiser and 20-inches.

But his team boss said: 'No! I'm placing you back to last.' It was terrible.

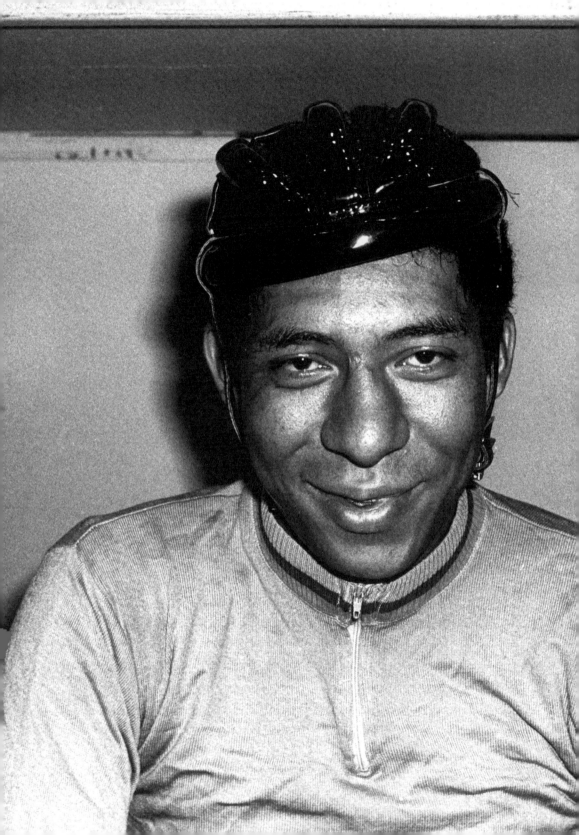

Charlie Reynolds leads the mens final at the Ipswich EBA National at Landseer Park in Ipswich, UK, 1991

It sat raw with me for a very long time. I actually gave up the sport for a while because of it. For me, every time I had the number two on my plate on my bike, it hurt and made me angry. That is why I always used to have number one on the side of my helmet. Because I was the Champion of Champions in Britain.

Tim Erwin reflects on similar experiences of white scrutiny.

At a crit in Pensacola, Florida, I was a junior racing in the senior race. I won and threw my arms up crossing the line. They [the commissaires] were going to DQ me for that. It took my white team-mate getting in the official's face for him to back down.

An even stronger verification of the black racing cyclist's experience of white commissaire bias comes from Justin Williams.

My second year at track nationals I had nothing but problems. I got relegated from Keirin. But it was somebody leaning on me! I had the race line. I was on the black line. Someone kept coming down on me, so I flicked them, and I got disqualified. That was weird.

In the match sprint final, I won the first one, but lost the second one. I thought I had won the third one just on the line.

But the judges wouldn't show me and my dad the finish line video of the race.

Then in the team sprint we were disqualified because I was told that I pulled up from the sprinter line too early. We won by about two seconds.

It was the first time I thought: 'Are these people racists?' I don't hold grudges. I felt some of the decisions were because of me being a black kid. I have dealt with racist people for my entire life. The only thing I can do is ignore them. But I was a kid and I was robbed of two national titles.

***

I walked over to see the chief commissaire, but in my mind I sensed that a big joke was being played on me, and I was going through its motions.

I passed Keith Butler, the co-organiser of the race along with Glyn. "Don't let him get to you!" he said as I walked by.

The chief commissaire got out of his car.

"Right! What was your number?" he said to me.

"Number one," I said.

"Yes. You. You're disqualified, for dangerous riding – crossing over the white line."

"What? There were actually quite a few other riders ahead of me that were doing that."

"But I only saw you, and you're disqualified."

"Are you sure it was me?"

"Yes! You stand out."

I turned immediately and walked away. 'Fuck it!' I whispered to myself. Everyone knew that I had won the race. I had been congratulated by some of the riders. But now the result didn't stand.

I walked past the podium prize ceremony. The London Dynamo riders who had finished behind me in the sprint were receiving their awards, shaking hands, hugging, smiling, and giggling with each other and having their photographs taken.

I got in my car and drove away. I didn't compete in many other road races after that. I had been outsprinting and beating elite road riders in my race wins, so I focused my attention on becoming a track sprinter instead.

CHAPTER 8 SHOW US YOUR TEETH

AT THE MEDAL CEREMONY WHEN I WAS HOLDING THE FLOWERS, SOME PEOPLE IN THE CROWD WERE BOOING. IT WASN'T SOMETHING THAT SURPRISED ME. IT WAS BECAUSE OF THE COLOUR OF MY SKIN
MAURICE BURTON

I liked Antony Stirrat. He was a
nice man. Always having fun, and not
taking things too seriously at the track.
It wasn't until years later that
I discovered he had taken part in the
1992 Olympics. That's cycling for you.
New riders can end up racing in the
same events and races as former pros,
former Olympians, current pros,
current Olympians without sometimes
even knowing it. Not many other
sports can offer the same challenge.
It was Antony who introduced me
to David Le Grys. David and Antony
had worked together on the Great
Britain cycling team, and David
became the first cycling coach I'd ever
worked with. In 2007 I won all of my
sprint races at the spring omnium races
at Herne Hill Velodrome, and so
I began to take part in the National
Sprinters League races. I won some
races there too. I loved sprinting.

It fitted with my physique. I wished I'd found it when I'd first entered the sport. And while David's 'Gimme All' turbo sessions nearly killed me, they worked. I won medals at regional, national and European track championships.

My first and only appearance racing the match sprint at world championship level was 2010 in Anadia, Portugal. David encouraged me to enter. I was working as a teacher at the time but the event fell during the school half-term holidays, so I entered.

I decided that I would wear British Cycling national colours in my races. The red, white, and blue would become my national skinsuit. It was a big decision for me. Why? Well, I wasn't selected to ride for Great Britain. But by entering this international competition, I had selected to represent Great Britain.

I was having a great season of racing. I had been on the podium at the European Masters Championships in Manchester that year with two other Brits. We watched the union flag go up to the national anthem.

All of this was a new weirdness for me. I felt a bit uncomfortable about what I was thinking about doing yet wanted to do it. I was very aware of my minority ethnic identity and presence in a white-dominated sport, and across the different generations of cyclists that I was meeting in my travels around the country. But I was above that thinking at the same time. I knew too that among the British team going to Portugal – which included former Olympians, former pros, and respected former champions at senior elite and masters level – I'd be the only black British rider.

I got the national skinsuit.

I tried it on. I felt great, and I looked great. I practised in it. It felt it gave me extra power.

I went to Portugal.

I wasn't the only rider to turn up for warm up sessions wearing the GB kit. But I noticed a few heads turning at me. A Scotsman came out from the melee and over to me. He began to talk about the event, and some other things, but one thing I remember him saying was something about "the significance and meaning of the jersey on my back". I didn't really know who he was, and I wasn't really listening. But at some points it felt like I was being subjected to the cycling equivalent of Norman Tebbit's 'cricket test'. Tebbit, a government minister under Margaret Thatcher, once argued that asking second generation immigrants whether they supported England in cricket was key to gauging their loyalty to the country and their degree of assimilation. Was this Scotsman warning me about something, or even trying to persuade me to take the skinsuit off? I couldn't. For one thing, I didn't have any other racing kit spare.

Questions of national identity, national allegiance, flying the flag for Great Britain have been put in the minds to test black cyclists. For example, Tre Whyte reflects on his encounters with this sense of white scrutiny.

I wasn't selected to go to the World Championships. The reason I was told was that I didn't hit my targets. There were five spots available to race in the Worlds and I wasn't allowed to fill one of those spots. I knew that if I went to the World Championships and if I did well, we could have got three spots for the Olympic Games. But I still wasn't allowed to go to the Worlds.

The sense that I got from them was that I was an embarrassment to them when they said: 'For you to pull on this jersey... ' and this and that. But I'd been wearing the jersey with pride all the time. I had already earned my spot, because of my performances in the previous year. I did well at the World Cup events. Anyway, they didn't let me go. So that was my Olympic shot done.

Maurice Burton's experience with the national kit was remarkably similar.

After I won the British championship in 1974, I went to the Awards Dinner in Blackpool to collect my trophy. I informed some of the British Cycling Federation officials there that I had been invited to race in Trinidad and Barbados in early 1975. Their reaction to me was: 'We didn't select you, so you won't be able to wear a Great Britain jersey.' I was a bit taken aback. There were going to be world class riders in this event. Their reaction didn't deter me from going. It was in the West Indies, and it was an all-expenses paid trip.

At 19, I am afraid I couldn't refuse it.

So I went there, and I won a couple of races. The one race which was quite memorable for me was where I beat a Frenchman called Daniel Morelon and a Danish rider called Niels Fredborg to win the race – and both of them were world and Olympic champions.

As I wasn't given a Great Britain jersey for the event, I wore my national champions jersey instead. I don't know why they said I couldn't wear their jersey. Maybe they thought I wasn't up to it. But that race proved otherwise.

I placed sixth in the 200m time trial sprint qualifier. I knew that
I could have gone quicker. I felt the track suited me. I was up against
a Russian rider in the first round. I beat him. In the best-of-three
quarterfinals, I had to race against the French champion. I beat him
too, in two rounds. I'd made it to the semi-finals. I was guaranteed
a ride for any one of the three medals.

At this point, the number of spectators in the velodrome was
growing. Some of the British riders and their families were seated
in the stands on the back straight, a very visible group. It was a great
feeling seeing them and, as the numbers grew, they became louder
and more talkative. I could hear them really clearly.

In the semi-finals, I squared up with the number two seed: the
South African champion. He had four tenths of a second on me
through the qualifying time trial. But I beat him. When I took the
second round in my semi-final clash, having been defeated in the first,
I was surprised to hear a roar from the Brits and the noise in the
velodrome. It was like nothing I had ever experienced. With all the
adrenaline in me, I looked up at the Brits and pumped my fist at them.
I'd never done anything like that before, but I was worked up.
They pumped their fists back. *Wow!* They were really with me.

As we approached the start line for the third round, I heard their
voices once more: "Come on, Marlon!", "Go on, Marlon!"

I was ready. I led out, jumping into the sprint higher up the track
and using my weight and power. There was no way around for him.
I crossed the line, mouth wide open, and ecstatic. I was shocked and
amazed at my performance. I could hear roars, big triumphant roars,
from the British contingent of the crowd. I had made a world
championship final.

I passed the Brits in the crowd on the back straight. I could see
them clapping, smiling, shouting, bowing, and waving. Again, I
pumped my fist as I passed them, and they punched the air back.

Then, suddenly, all the lights in the velodrome switched off.
Boom!! Boom!!!

We were all immediately plunged into pitch black. Something
had gone wrong. A power cut.

The noise in the velodrome immediately became more subdued.
I was rolling around the track on my bike, winding down but –
panting after my effort, my heart pumping – I became a bit anxious.
Would we have to do it again? Would that race result not stand?
The sudden blackout in the velodrome seemed a bad omen.

In the darkness, I heard a loud crack of laughter from the track centre.

I finally made it around to the gate. I got my breath back and made my way down the ramp to track centre. Moments later, the lights began to come back on, one by one. There were a few cheers, and people started to clap at this. I got off the bike, climbed on my turbo-trainer, and began warming down.

A Welsh rider came over to me.

"Awesome ride, Marlon!" he said.

I nodded in acknowledgement.

"Thanks. It was tough," I replied.

"But wasn't it funny though..." he added.

"Hmm. What?"

"When the lights went out, didn't you hear what Smithy shouted out?"

"No," I shrugged.

He grinned as he spoke: "'Hey, Marlon! Show us your teeth! We can't see your face down here!'"

Suddenly it became clear what the laughter in the track centre had been about. I had become the focus of a petty racist quip.

My experience is an example of the double-sided nature of acceptance and rejection for the black cycling athlete. I had received support and encouragement from the white British contingent. The power of the national skinsuit helped fuel it. For a moment, I was fully 'in' and I was one of them. They supported me, they embraced me, they cheered for me. Minutes later some of the very same people were also sharing in the laughter as my skin colour was mocked. I was quickly returned to be the other.

***

Once again, <u>Maurice Burton</u> had been there before me. He too experienced feeling accepted at times due to his abilities as a cyclist and then rejected at others, solely because of his skin colour. His 1974 season offers several particularly strong examples.

I beat the 10-mile race gold and silver medallists from the Commonwealth Games to win the British championships. I put four lengths into them. So, it was something that I felt good about. I was smiling. It was on television as well.

At the medal ceremony when I was holding the flowers, some people in the crowd were booing. It wasn't something that surprised me. It was because of the colour of my skin.

Again, the confusion imposed upon the black rider results from flitting between being included and excluded: the former through his quality and ability as a cyclist; the latter by a sense of racism used to diminish these traits. Maurice experienced similar treatment at the Commonwealth Games that year.

I was invited to some kind of garden party reception. It was for the local dignitaries and I think it was the Duke of Edinburgh who was representing the Royal Family in New Zealand at that time, he was going to be there. My name was the one that was supposed to be going. But when they [the coaches] saw that, I did not get to go. They sent somebody else instead. It was me that the organisers had requested attend.

At that age, I could not turn around and say: 'Listen, that's my name on the invitation and I'm going.' I could not do that at that stage. I just could not do it. I mean, I was only a young kid. I mean, a few months later, I beat the hell out of those guys anyway. You know, back in those days, when I was at training sessions, they used to call me a 'coon'.

The mixture of insidious and direct racism experienced by Maurice aimed to scar and disempower him. But it couldn't stop his desire and determination to reach his ultimate goal of becoming a professional cyclist. The skin of the black rider in the white world of competitive cycling is the subject of mockery, taunts, and scorn, and perhaps even more so when the rider within this skin displays ambition and delivers with excellence and grace in their endeavours as a racing cyclist.

Years later, Christian Lyte would also experience the pain of British coaches seeking to downplay his achievements.

Getting my individual world title was a big thing for me, the first one [the Keirin title at the world junior championships]. It was good, but it was not celebrated. Afterwards, it was like, 'got the medals and then back to the hotel and then straight back home'. It was not really celebrated fully in that moment. For me, it was like a massive achievement. But for our coach it was like: 'It's not that good. It's just a junior world title. Back in.' It wasn't deemed as a massive thing at the time.

I remember, it was me and Jess Varnish. We were putting our bikes away. We went to doping control. We came out of doping control and in Mexico, everybody wants your autograph. Track cycling is a massive thing for them and I don't think the world championships had been at that track before. The coach was in a rush and was shouting for us to come over, he said: 'It's just a junior world title. For God's sake, hurry up!' But they are hard individual titles to win.

In the face of continuing rejection from national selectors – either
not being called up at all, or being neglected once the call has come –
some black cyclists have experienced a watershed moment in their
career. It might mean hanging up their wheels entirely. Or it might
mean setting sail for new shores and investigating opportunities in
the lands of their forefathers.

CHAPTER 9
IT WASN'T GOING TO HAPPEN

ALL I CAN THINK OF NOW IS THAT IT WAS A RACIST DECISION. IF YOU ARE WHITE, YOU GET TO GO. IF YOU ARE BLACK, YOU GET TO STAY AT HOME. SAME THING. SAME STORY

RUSSELL WILLIAMS

Russell Williams takes a sponsorship break at the Milk Race in 1987

All young ambitious racing cyclists want to represent their national team. But for black cyclists, particularly in the USA and UK, it is a challenging and high stakes situation. "There are a smaller number of black riders racing bikes," explains Rahsaan Bahati. "If John Smith [the white rider] isn't selected for the team, his race [ethnic group] is still represented. But if you isolate it to us, we're a small number, now you can see the impact to a whole generation of black cyclists." Likewise Erik Saunders insinuates that his skin colour affected his chances. "Certain people weren't ever going to get a look by the national team, or you'd have to keep trying and trying to really stand out. I wasn't interested in playing that game. I accepted that others may place a ceiling on me."

Russell Williams prepared himself as the model professional; notably delivering the necessary national championship victories to demonstrate that he was number one in the country. The return for his hard work was being frozen out by national selectors for the opportunity to race and compete for Great Britain at the highest level.

In 1987 I wanted to go to the world championships. So at the start of the year I had a conversation with the national coaches and I said: 'What do I have to do to go to the worlds?' Because I was thinking: 'Worlds – Olympics'; it's always a stepping stone.

The national coach said to me: 'OK, Russell. You win the national championships, then you go to the worlds.'

Back then I wasn't full-time as a professional, I was working, I had a family. I did everything correct. I went to the national championships. I won the national championships in a British record time. That made me the best person in the UK.

Straight after the race, I went to see the coach. I said: 'Am I going to the world championships?'

He said to me: 'No. You're not going.'

I was hesitant, but I sort of asked him: 'Why?'

But he didn't answer the question. He was evasive. Even worse was to come. I found out that the riders behind me in second and third place [at the national championships] were selected instead of me to go and represent Great Britain at the world championships.

All I can think of now is that it was a racist decision. If you are white, you get to go. If you are black, you get to stay at home. Same thing. Same story. It was very disappointing. Due to who was there at the head of British Cycling at the time, there is no way I was going to get to ride. They made it uncomfortable for me. It was a like a boys' club. If the big boss director doesn't want you in, then what can you do? Grow another leg? What can you do? It's not possible, is it?

Russell's belief is that the difference in his skin colour from that of other cyclists has influenced decisions against him. Some people may seek to dismiss his sense of reality. But this would be an insult to his lived experience.

Maurice Burton speaks about how his fortunes changed with the departure of a national coach that had favoured him.

Norman Sheil was the national coach and he sent me to the Commonwealth Games in 1974. However, through politics and everything else, by the time we got to the Commonwealth Games, Norman was no longer the coach. He and the Federation [British Cycling] parted company. He went over to Canada. From those Commonwealth Games onwards, I never got selection to ride for this country again. Never.

David Clarke racing at the Eddie Soens Memorial race at Aintree in 2012

Down the generations, showing top form and being the best of the best has generally been insufficient for the black British cyclist to gain attention from the national coach and a spot on the national team, as David Clarke explains.

I'd done national squad training. I was selected to ride for Great Britain in an international cyclo-cross event in Dover as an under-23 age group rider. I won that race. There was another race coming up, and I was hoping to ride for Great Britain again at the inter-area cyclo-cross championships in Hurstpierpoint. But I was surprised not to be picked for that team.

You know, I'd won the last 15 or so races that I had been in. Yet I wasn't picked. They [the coaches] said they wanted to give everybody else a chance. But this chance was for the older riders. I was the youngest rider on the team at the time and I was winning and beating them. I guess that was part of the reason why I'd had enough of cyclo-cross.

It wasn't the first time David didn't receive a selection he felt his results had earned him.

I had won the Junior Tour of Wales which was a 'guaranteed' spot to the world junior road race championships

and I still didn't get selected. It's a bitter pill to take. Nobody really gave me a reason why I did not go.

These experiences echo those of Cory Williams. Despite a string of impressive results, he would still be ignored for national selection.

I've been one of the top cyclists in America – even the best at my age at one point. I've been national champion, won a stage race overall, won a green jersey, won over 20 state championships and been top 20 at national road races as a junior and never been able to represent America on the national team.

In 2020, Cory Williams did finally get a chance to ride for his country when he was selected to represent the USA in the Zwift ESports World Championships.

His compatriot Rahsaan Bahati also had the experience of wearing the stars and stripes – early in his career, he was chosen for the national junior and espoir teams, representing the USA at races around the world. Still, he feels that the rules for his gaining selection were different to those for other riders.

Rahsaan Bahati at the Manhattan Beach Grand Prix in 2009

They told me I had to win the junior road race at nationals if I wanted to be selected for worlds. I had been winning races all year, but I have to win? I won the race solo, but what if I had gotten second?

It's similar for Tre Whyte. He sensed that he was being ridiculed by national coaches during his mid-career experiences.

There was a time when I felt mocked, when I said: 'You didn't let me race for a chance to get to the Olympics.' But this was after I had been told: 'Well, you can still go if, by three weeks from now, you can beat this time by three-tenths of a

Cory Williams in his California State champion's jersey. He and brother Justin are founding members of the Legion of LA (L39ION) race team

second from the top to the bottom of a hill.' That was going to be impossible. Maybe three-hundredths. But to be given three weeks to beat a time by three-tenths to the bottom of the hill? Impossible. That's the kind of stuff that I was told that I needed to do. They knew. They didn't want me there. Whatever. I was on a high streak for 2014/15 and then I crashed. It meant that I was a bit inconsistent in the 2016 season, but I still ended up making it to the World Cup Finals. So, it was quite harsh to be hearing that I was going to kicked off the BMX squad. Even when my times were quicker than others, I would still be overlooked for selection.

Charlotte Cole-Hossain has a similar tale to tell.

In my personal opinion sometimes I have been not picked for things which I think I should have deserved to get on to. When I was going into my second year of racing as an under-16 rider, British Cycling introduced a programme called the ODA [Olympic Development Apprentices]. It was a programme for 15- and 16-year-olds. It was supposed to be open to 40 girls and 40 boys from across the country.

I was fairly certain that I was going to get on, based upon my results from the year before and my overall career record including as a double national champion. I'd come fifth in the national madison championships. I thought that result at least would be enough to be considered for the top 40 girls in the country. I didn't get chosen for that.

I did think that there may be other reasons [beyond racial bias] why, and that it might be that they didn't like my attitude, or they didn't think that I was hard working enough or something. It was quite difficult for me at the time. I missed out on getting the best training support system in the country.

Everyone could say: 'I deserved to be this. I deserved to be that' and a lot of the time they probably don't. People get picked based upon how good they are and what they can bring to the team. I just thought that specific programme, I think that I could have probably been a better rider, had I been involved in that programme.

Charlotte Cole-Hossain at the National Track Championships in Manchester 2017

Another young black British rider, Caelan Miller, vividly remembers the same sort of exclusion.

Through my high-ranking position in the national series I would have thought I should have been considered for coaching under the British Cycling National School of Racing, but I was excluded over racers who at the time had not beaten me. This was the first time that I realised your accomplishments were not necessarily going to be a guarantee of inclusion with the British Cycling organisation. In the end that had a definite negative effect on me.

For Russell Williams, a consistent lack of selection by the national team provides some of the most painful memories from his cycling career, not least when a British team representative admitted why they'd previously overlooked him.

One big thing for me that I remember is when one their masseurs once said to me while I was on the table: 'Russell, I'm so sorry.'

I said: 'What are you sorry about?'

He said: 'Not picking you all those years. I heard from people that while you were racing abroad you must have been taking things. But now I know you weren't.'

For me, hearing that was like a knife through the heart. I'd been blocked from possible selection to the 1984 Olympics.

When you are winning and beating everyone who is being selected over you, you think: 'How much more do I have to do?'

Ultimately, it was an experience that drove him away from his home country.

I dominated as much as I could. But I was just not getting selected. So, I thought: 'What is the next move? OK. Go to America and race, earn a bit of money, and then come back and win the nationals.' So they will go: 'Hang on, Russell should be in the team.'

In 1995 I won the national madison title with Rob Hayles. The director of British Cycling at the time had said to me: 'If you win the nationals with Rob, you're guaranteed a ride at Manchester to do the world championships for Britain.'

Well, at the time we had the fastest 50km. We were a super team. We knew how to ride. I was flying with Rob. Well, we won the race, but after that, they just flicked me. I didn't get a look in. They said: 'No. You can't ride.'

They offered the ride to Rob and somebody else. They promised me something there, but I didn't get it.

Russell's frustrations were nothing new to the black British cyclist. Maurice Burton went through the same process of selection denial.

Russell Williams racing at Herne Hill, London for the VCL team in 1987

1976 was Olympic year, so I came back to England with the hope that I could come on to the team. So around Easter, I raced in the UK and I beat them all. I beat the guys. You know, it was an embarrassment. You know, the newspapers were starting to get involved in this. They were asking: 'What's going on? How could this guy? Why isn't he even on the squad?' Because there were guys on that squad [who] I don't think had even won a race.

So they had to take me into the squad, and I went through the processes. But I knew pretty much that it wasn't going to work, it wasn't going to happen. I just knew. I could see that some guys fitted, whilst I didn't. And these were guys who weren't getting the same results in big events like I had been.

For me, the reason for wanting to go to the Olympics Games was because at that time it was for amateurs, not for professionals. If you could get a good result, then you could turn professional. You could come in on a higher [salary] level. I had to come in at a lower level than those guys, because I didn't have those qualifications. I wanted that qualification, but I couldn't get it.

Later on I did hold a Jamaican passport. What I should have done was gone down that avenue for international racing opportunities.

Through a desire to address the denial and discrimination they have experienced, riders like Tre Whyte have shown a resolute determination to take things into their own hands; to shape their own destiny.

I have had some big barriers and I have felt like quitting. I wasn't selected to go the 2014 Worlds. So I paid my own way. I went over to Rotterdam. Somebody crashed into the British rider Liam Phillips in the eighth-final race. So he went out the competition. I went on to the final and got world number three.

That was a big story at the time.

I wasn't officially selected to go and represent Great Britain, but I paid my own way and got a bronze medal. For me it was kind of like: 'In your face!'

Nothing much was said to me about it afterwards, to be honest. I got a 'well done'. But that was it.

In 2016, I wasn't selected again, but this time they didn't even let me pay my own way to go.

Frustrations with the selection process for the Great Britain team have sometimes led black British cyclists to consider competing for the country of their father's birth instead. Christian Lyte had three world junior track sprint championships under his belt when he considered taking such a route, believing British Cycling was serving to stymie his potential.

I should have been selected for more World Cup races. But I didn't get to ride any of those races in Great Britain colours. None. I was never selected. Others were selected and our times on the track were very comparable. I became frustrated. I think at that point I did get in contact with the Barbadian track cyclist Barry Forde via social media.

Christian Lyte wins a silver medal in the Keirin at the European Track Championships in Cottbus, Germany, 2007

Having won a string of quality professional UCI Continental races, David Clarke enquired further into his paternal links with Jamaica.

I would no longer be British if I went down that route, and I was riding for Endura at the time who already had a lot of foreign riders. It would have made it hard for me to continue to ride for them, as they needed to have a balance of foreign and British riders. So that put me off going with Jamaica. On reflection, I definitely should have gone with them. It would have been a world platform for me.

Russell Williams also talks of turning down alternative international opportunities.

In 1983 and 1984, I was winning big races in the USA. The USA director of cycling said: 'I want to pick you for our Olympic team.' I said: 'Well of course, I can't,' being British. At that point, I contacted my father's country of birth Trinidad and Tobago and considered riding for them at the 1984 Olympics. But it was difficult with paperwork and letter writing. I guess I left it a bit late as well.

As a junior rider, Russell did race for Team GB in the 1977 and 1978 World Championships. As a senior, he won 18 national championships. But he only once competed internationally for his

country: at the 1987 World Championships in Vienna, where he finished a respectable sixth in the points race.

Being continually overlooked or denied opportunities to ride for the national team is not an experience shared by all black cyclists. France has produced many outstanding black riders who have worn the national colours. Yavé Cahard took silver in the match sprint at the 1980 summer Olympics and world championship medals in 1982, 1983 and 1984. On his shoulders stands Grégory Baugé, the four-time Olympic medallist and nine-time world sprint champion. More recently, Marie-Divine Kouamé Taky become a junior world sprint champion, and Kévin Reza has represented France in the world road race championships. Apart from a few world championship track appearances by BMX rider Shanaze Reade in 2007 and 2008, black British cyclists have been largely absent. So how come France can do this for its black road and track cycling athletes, but Great Britain has not? Why do so many black British cyclists feel so marginalised they have to consider opportunities in countries other than their own?

There has never been a black rider who has represented Great Britain at Olympic road or track cycling events. It seems to me that some of those who have entered white-dominated spaces at the highest levels of the sport – those who could have been selected but were sidelined by national coaches – have been left frustrated by a claim associated with white British nationalism: 'There ain't no black in the Union Jack.'

CHAPTER 10
ADVENTURE AND SURVIVAL

I WAS GOING TO HAVE A BIG CAREER RACING IN EUROPE. I WASN'T THE FASTEST. I WASN'T THE STRONGEST. BUT I HAD RACE CRAFT INTELLIGENCE WHICH WOULD HELP ME GET TO THE FINISH LINE COMPETING FOR THE WIN

RAHSAAN BAHATI

Rahsaan Bahati rode for the Mercury Cycling Team in the USA from 2000 to 2002

When Maurice Burton realised he wasn't going to make it onto the British team for the 1976 Olympics, he made a big decision: to largely end his days of racing in the nation of his birth. "I just left and went to Belgium. I never bothered to come back and race here again, apart from certain events, certain big events. I'd been to Belgium the winter before in 1974 and the promoter Oscar Daemars wanted me to come back to ride in the Six Day event. I'd never ridden in a professional Six Day event before that. By the Christmas of that year, I was riding with the professionals, with Eddy Merckx and all of those guys. I was 19 years old. I rode my first race as a professional on Christmas Day in Ghent."

In due course, <u>Russell Willliams</u> would make the same journey.

I took the ferry over and took the train to Ghent. The ferry got there early, at about 7am. After docking, I rang Maurice and woke him – he was still in bed sleeping.

But we arranged to meet a few hours after that. He was the only rider up there in the sport who was a black British man. There were no other black cyclists.

Two young black men from the concrete jungle of South London, together testing the truth of their ambitions by riding and competing against some of the best riders in the world. Both were outliers, as <u>Maurice</u> explains.

Somebody put a picture on Facebook the other day, and some guy asked me: 'Is this you?' I said: 'Who else do you think it could be?' You see, there was nobody else out there, no other black riders.

Moving to Belgium enabled <u>Maurice</u> to really show what he was capable of – to overcome some of the obstacles placed in his way when in Britain – but also to make a living from the sport he loved. Even so, there were many compromises to be made.

My reason for turning professional was partly to ride on the road, but the main thing for me was the Six Day racing. What I could earn in those Six Days and one event, some riders wouldn't even make that in a year on the road. I used to walk away from a Six Day event with £2,000 a week. And that kind of money, it was very hard to do that on the road.

I remember a Belgian rider, Etienne De Wilde, who had ridden in the Tour de France. He made more money in the Ghent Six Day than he did in the Tour de France.

I was recently talking with Johan Museeuw, the former world road race champion; multiple winner of Paris-Roubaix. He is from the west of Flanders and he had riders from his team that were from Antwerp. And because they were from Antwerp and he was from West Flanders, they wouldn't ride for him.

Now, you just imagine, someone like me in a team over there, a black guy. Could you ever see those guys riding for me? I don't think so! So I knew that the team thing on the road wasn't really going to work for me.

<u>Maurice</u> knew that survival in Belgium meant playing the game in a world where local riders are always favoured. He took the money and support when it came, whether that was agreeing to be the Madison partner of the Belgian rider Dirk Herwig – under payment by Herwig's father – or gifting a race to Eddy Merckx.

It was just the two of us left at the end of an elimination race. I'd already beaten him that night, so he knew that I was very keen. He came alongside me and had little word in my ear. He said: 'Will you let me win this one?' I said: 'OK, Eddy.'

There were some great highs for <u>Maurice</u>, including teaming up with fellow British rider Paul Medhurst to beat Merckx and his partner in the Ghent Six Day points race. But these were coupled with the lows. At one event he was almost poisoned, the result of a cocktail of substances he'd unknowingly been given by a soigneur he had previously trusted.

And in Belgium, too, there was a periodic reminder that he could not escape special attention being given to his blackness in this white-dominated space.

Some Australians and British amateurs ganged up against me at the Ghent Six. One of them tried to put me over the rail. I knew exactly what was happening. Afterwards I went down into one of the massage cabins underneath the track. I wrecked the cabin with the guy in it.

The outburst led to a one-month racing ban. Yet the gang of riders that aimed to cause him a life-threatening injury carried on racing freely the next day.

Then there was the time <u>Maurice</u> travelled to Vienna, where he would be line up against Patrick Sercu – a master of the Six Day.

When I arrived, I saw the newspaper, and one of the sports page headlines read: 'Can the Nigger beat Sercu?' Now can you imagine what sort of people were going to be in that crowd? The velodrome was owned by a former SS officer who was the father of an Austrian rider.

Maurice raced 56 times as a professional Six Day rider, all across the Europe and the world. His adventures are unique, his survival astonishing.

***

The <u>David Clarke</u> odyssey is another unique story of adventure. He gives an account of his travels and racing across the world. This was to some extent an enforced wandering caused by him being unable to secure private funding or racing contracts with leading British racing teams, despite his outstanding cycling ability. But his journeying, although tough, is something he seems to have enjoyed.

I joined teams where I thought the racing would be best and where I'd stand the best chance of getting a place. Initially, I had struggled to get a place on the Dave Rayner Fund, and so in 2001 I eventually just went off my own back and joined a smallish team in France called UCD Nord 87, based right in the middle of France. I had a year there. It was started by a British guy called Laurence Brown. He had quite a lot of influence in it.

In 2002, I went to the Athletic Club de Boulogne-Billancourt which I guess is like a French amateur club. A lot of famous British and English-speaking riders like Robert Millar, Sean Yates, Phil Anderson and Steven Roche had been there in the past. Probably any British road cyclist that had made it went to that club.

I had some time after that in Spain. But it got a bit complicated. This was an era when cycling wasn't as clean as maybe it is now. Anyway, there was pressure put on me to take stuff. In the end, I agreed not to take anything but to ride for no money. So then I wasn't getting paid and I had to rent my own flat.

It was a time when Endura [were setting up] a British team based in Italy. So, at the end of May in that year, I switched teams and joined them.

With Endura, I was always riding with and against the biggest professional teams out there at the time. If you got around and finished in the top 20, that would have been a really good ride. In the 2003 GP Schwarzwald, I remember [2011 Tour de France winner] Cadel Evans blowing hard and telling me not ride so hard on the climbs.

There were one or two riders from Columbia racing in Italy but in that era I don't remember seeing any African or Caribbean riders. None.

In 2003, 2004, Endura finished and so I moved to a French team, Le Creusot. Then in 2005, I rode in Guadeloupe. There were a lot of Caribbean riders over there. The racing over there was a big scene. Every race was hilly. Most races were on the same island with a big climb in it. You could kind of guess what the result would be. I would generally be in the top 10 every time.

I have raced all over world: South America, USA, El Salvador, China, Taiwan, Malaysia, Borneo, Indonesia, New Zealand. I have raced in pretty much all of the European countries.

In 2009 I won race after race: King of the Mountains in the Tour of Romania; the Grand Prix Chantel Biya in Cameroon; the Tour de Okinawa in Japan.

I rode abroad for most of my career so I wasn't really racing in front of my friends and family. So the East Yorkshire Classic in 2010 was a nice win for me because it was at home. I put my arms up in the air with my mum standing by the finish line, and in front of an English crowd.

The good results continued for <u>David</u>. In 2012, he was the best placed home rider at the Tour of Britain and also took the King of the Mountains title in the Tour of Ireland. Yet he still couldn't land what he most wanted.

I had got some good results, but for the next year in 2013, I struggled to attract a good British team.

He wound up riding that season for Baku, a team from Azerbaijan.

Beats me why I couldn't get myself a British team for 2013. It's hard to put your finger on it and know why. But I faced that quite a lot in my career, where I thought my results were perhaps better than the teams that I rode for. Being a black man probably didn't help. But also I wasn't French, I wasn't Spanish, I wasn't Italian, and I wasn't prepared to take drugs. These also probably hampered my prospects, especially when I was in Spain.

Cycling teams tend to be funded by one person with a lot of money who has a passion for the sport that take people on that they particularly like themselves.

Christian Lyte of Barbados in Aguadilla, Puerto Rico during the XXI Central American and Caribbean Games, 2010

***

<u>Christian Lyte</u> was just 19 when he found out that – despite being a triple world junior champion and having taken European and national titles – his time with British Cycling had already come to an end.

I always felt that I was being side-lined. I received a letter thanking me for my time and service. I was asked to leave within a month.

When I came off the squad, I managed to be able to train and race for Barbados. I left England and went to Berlin in Germany, where the Barbados team was based. I was in contact with their coach Barry Forde for a while. I messaged him and said: 'Look, this is what is happening. But I have got heritage through my father and if I get some citizenship, what is the deal? Could I come and train with you guys?' He welcomed me without hesitation.

I began training with those guys.

I went over to the Caribbean to race in the Central American and Caribbean Games in Puerto Rico. I was supposed to go on to the Commonwealth Games in 2010 but I didn't manage to get my citizenship through on time. So that was when things with Barbados began to finish.

The last race that I did in my career was the national Keirin championships in 2009. It was a big one. My lead up to it wasn't going great. My training was not specific [to the event]. I didn't have the help, as I was out of the Barbados and British squads at that point. But I still got the bronze. It was a very tight and twitchy race with Chris Hoy and Jason

Motivated, professional and fast. The Williams brothers are changing the way the media views black cyclists for the better

Kenny just inches ahead of me in the end. Chris and Jason were current Olympic champions. I beat Matt Crampton and Dave Daniell who were both riders I had worked with before but had been retained on the British squad. I beat the best of all the other riders in the country.

It was like confirmation that even off the squad I was good enough, and that I shouldn't have had to come off. I think that bronze medal in the last race I did was my biggest achievement. For me, it symbolises how unfair it was. I think at that moment, it was bigger than a world title; being on the podium with Chris and Jason.

***

For <u>Rahsaan Bahati</u>, it was a nationally-based opportunity that saw him ride overseas. But inadequate support meant it was a shortlived experience.

As a junior, I got on to the national team and spent a lot of time in Belgium where the USA national team house is. I also spent some time in Spain. I really thought that I was going to have a big career racing in Europe. I wasn't the fastest; I wasn't the strongest. There were some early kickings. But I adapted. I had race craft intelligence which would help me get to the finish line competing for the win. I raced in the Junior Tour of Flanders; Junior Paris-Roubaix; French Cup races.

I was always in there. I thought: 'One of these days, I will win one of these things.' I raced the Junior Worlds in Plouay, France. I was not one of the favourites, but I was having such a good race, and believe it or not, on the uphill there was a crash which I ran into. It was not a big deal. I grabbed my bike to get up; to get back into the pack. I was in the lead pack, and then my seat fell off. I had the rails, but no saddle. So, I rushed to the pit, but there was not a spare bike for me. So, it was game over. That race stands out for me, because the guy who won on that day was from New Zealand, Jeremy Yates. All year long, I was beating Jeremy. There are no regrets. It was his day. Phillipe Gilbert was in that race; Marcel Sieberg; André Greipel. We are all the same age. None of them got on the podium. It just goes to show that you need to stay in for long enough, and put in the work. Looking back, I wish I had more support from USA Cycling and from my team to keep me over there. I thought I could have a good splash, but it just didn't happen.

***

Culture shock has often been described by riders who have left their home countries to try and make it in the sport. But for Justin Williams, the colour of his skin added to the problems in settling in and acclimatising.

Rahsaan Bahati riding for the Mercury team in 2001

In Europe I was called 'difficult'. They called me a charity case and stereotyped me as an angry black man. I was written off faster than other riders and watched a lot of guys get on teams that never won a race. As a black man from the 'hood, I was typecast before managers even got to know me.

Williams talks about the European representation of what it means to be a professional cyclist.

That's something that I've struggled with my whole career, wanting to be myself, wanting to bring the culture that I grew up with into a sport without feeling like I'm going to get judged.

Williams returned to the USA and recalibrated his vision of cycling. Along with his brother Cory, he founded L39ION of Los Angeles – a UCI Continental cycling team which has the explicit goal of increasing diversity and inclusion in cycling. In 2018 and 2019, Justin won back-to-back national criterium championships in the team's colours.

The time is now! We are taking control of our own destiny. The team is building a future where everyone is welcome. The reimagining of cycling has started and it has a new face.

He added that "L39ION doesn't force riders to conform to white norms", though its roster consists of riders of all ethnicities and races. In trying to address the overwhelming whiteness of the sport, that isn't an approach being taken by all black cyclists.

CHAPTER 11 THE VELODROME OF WHITENESS

In the last 20 years cycling in Britain has been enjoying a golden age, both as a cultural activity and a spectator sport. This is underlined by figures from the national body British Cycling. In August 2016, its website reported a 700% increase in membership: up from 15,000 members in 2005 to 125,000 – 75,000 of them having joined since the London Olympics in 2012. In 2019, the website announced membership had reached 150,000 for the first time, a three-fold increase since 2012. Cycling's impact on the British public's consciousness has been acknowledged by six-time Olympic track sprint champion Sir Chris Hoy. "The British Cycling of 2019 is absolutely unrecognisable from that of 2000. Through the endeavours of our elite riders and coaches and the boom in support and enthusiasm from the British public, cycling now enjoys a much more prominent place in the national consciousness."

This recognition of "the boom in support and enthusiasm" and "through the endeavours of our elite riders and coaches" can be used as a starting point to analyse the increased popularity of competitive road racing and track cycling in 21st century Britain.

Multiple successes on the track and road in the 2004 Athens and 2008 Beijing Olympic Games stimulated the growth of public interest in cycling. Perhaps the greatest sense of pride in Great Britain's competitive cycling achievements during this 'golden age' came in 2012, when (Sir) Bradley Wiggins became Britain's first ever Tour de France winner.

Following his seminal victory, the internationally-renowned, British-led professional cycling team Team Sky (now INEOS Grenadiers) has won the Tour de France on five further occasions, through Chris Froome (four victories) and Geraint Thomas (one). The squad has also claimed two editions of the Vuelta a España (Chris Froome in 2011, awarded retrospectively, and in 2017) and two editions of the Giro d'Italia (Froome in 2018 and Tao Geoghegan Hart in 2020).

All of this British success has been under the leadership of Sir David Brailsford, firstly as performance director at British Cycling and then as team principal at Sky/INEOS Grenadiers.

The London Olympics of 2012 provided Brailsford and his team an opportune platform for a show of world dominance.

It seemed to me as though the BBC coverage of the 2012 Olympic Games was fully anchored from the London velodrome. Based on previous Olympic successes in track cycling, Britain's national public service broadcaster must have predicted that was where the nation could be drawn together to be enthused by the triumphs of its cycling heroes and heroines.

Members of the British establishment such as the Duke and Duchess of Cambridge were in attendance, anticipating victories for the nation amongst the vigorous waving of British union flags.

Great Britain was fuelled to glory in what I remember as a 'velodrome of whiteness'; roaring waves of white faces and union flags galore, creating an atmosphere of British patriotism similar to that seen during the Last Night of the Proms at London's Royal Albert Hall. This was a home Olympics for Great Britain, so the reaction was perhaps not unexpected.

Following the Games, a host of awards was bestowed upon the country's Olympic and Paralympic cyclists and their coaches, including knighthoods, damehoods and a plethora of honours such as MBEs, OBEs and CBEs. (Sir) Chris Hoy, (Sir) Bradley Wiggins, (Dame) Sarah Storey and (Sir) David Brailsford all benefitted. This raised their public statuses as national sports heroes.

It wasn't just white British Olympic heroes and heroines who were honoured. The black British athletes (Dame) Jessica Ennis and (Sir) Mohamed Farah also received titles. Still, the greater value and popularity given to white British cyclists is evidenced by the sequence of road and track riders who won the revered, publicly-voted, BBC Sports Personality of the Year award. In 2008 it was won by Sir Chris Hoy; Mark Cavendish took the honours in 2011; Sir Bradley Wiggins in 2012; and Geraint Thomas in 2018.

Of course, Dame Jessica Ennis and Sir Mohamed Farah have both also won this award, as has the black Formula One driver Lewis Hamilton.

From 2008 to 2016, there was a conveyor belt of road and track cyclists (all white) nominated for the award: Chris Froome OBE, Victoria Pendleton CBE, Dame Sarah Storey, Laura Kenny (née Trott) CBE and Jason Kenny CBE, demonstrating the extent of cycling's popularity with the public.

There have been clear examples of how elite cycling success in Britain over the last 10 years has been portrayed through exclusive communications of whiteness. British cyclists elevated to greater public knowledge and appeal have been fuelled by communications of white British nostalgia.

The media and commercial lionising of Bradley Wiggins as a professional cyclist represented as a Mod connects one recent 'golden age' of Britain (cycling success) to another nostalgic 'golden age' of Britain's past – the 'Swinging Sixties'. Mods have popular appeal to generations of white British people through the public images of musicians from white British rock bands such as: The Who in the 1960s; and later on The Jam in the 1980s; and Oasis during the 1990s/2000s. The superficial representation of a cycling superstar framed in this way connected with white British cultural sensibilities.

I remember when I was younger how my white school friends had older brothers who were Mods. They were alright. I had no issues with them, and I even remember lending them my father's Prince Buster ska records. But in my view, black British people cannot be Mods. This is an exclusive white British identity and subculture.

In 2012, I was on the Champs-Élysées with thousands of British fans to see Bradley Wiggins in the Tour de France yellow jersey leading out Mark Cavendish in the world champion's rainbow jersey.

THERE HAVE BEEN CLEAR EXAMPLES OF HOW ELITE CYCLING SUCCESS IN BRITAIN OVER THE LAST 10 YEARS HAS BEEN PORTRAYED THROUGH EXCLUSIVE COMMUNICATIONS OF WHITENESS

For a British cycling fan, this was just too unique an occurrence to miss.

Well, on the day, there were certainly a lot more British people than when I first came to the Tour de France finale in 1994. If there were some British people then, I didn't notice them. But I did this time. British Cycling's new 'barmy army' with their stick-on Mod sideburns, colonising the cafés and the side streets with their union flags wrapped around their waists and shoulders. This was the beginning of British Grand Tour domination by David Brailsford and Team Sky (now INEOS Grenadiers). In the present white British cultural attitude of world domination, the past remains.

In Great Britain's golden age of cycling, Sir Bradley Wiggins the cyclist became 'King of the Mods' and British Cycling's messiah. He will continue to be celebrated for his 2012 successes and is a cycling legend. But was it only me who saw how British patriotism mutated to become a drunken and exclusionary celebration of cycling through nostalgia and ethnic nationalism?

Another example was the portrayal of 2012 Olympic track sprint champion Victoria Pendleton. She was marketed to the British public through a representation of 'Britannia' – the female embodiment of Great Britain as empire and ruler of the world. She was also promoted to the British public in a remake of Ridley Scott's 1973 TV advert for bread company Hovis, 'Boy on a Bike'. Pendleton appeared in traditional English costume as the girl on the bicycle making deliveries of brown bread whilst riding through the quintessential English thatched roof cottage village of Shaftesbury in Dorset. Can you imagine a black girl dressed up this way, or as Britannia? White British traditionalists would be aghast.

These constructed media and commercial representations of Bradley Wiggins and Victoria Pendleton project culturally nostalgic representations of the white British self. In my view, these commercial uses of white British cycling superstars reinforced a normative taken-for-granted cultural association and ownership of cycling. It said: 'Here are our present heroes and heroines of elite road and track cycling as symbolic representations of our white British cultural past.' This is a message tied to history, heritage, tradition, in which the British Empire is resurrected, creating a power dynamic of racial and ethnic segregation.

I am in no doubt that the success achieved by Great Britain's national cycling team, and by white British professional riders, has been absolutely phenomenal. However, I take a perspective that the recent successes of Great Britain communicated through exclusive white British cultural discourses, nostalgic and triumphant representations of empire have amplified competitive cycling (particularly road and track) as an exclusive domain of white British ownership.

Where the context, representation and status of road and track cycling in Britain is portrayed in this way – through familiarity of culture, and a sense of connection and belonging – it seems to me that the attraction and cultural reproduction of white British elite and professional cyclists is likely to occur more rapidly than the growth and production of black British elite and professional cyclists.

White British cyclists are given a sense of entitlement where they see the history of their people portrayed through their sport and culture. All 'other' ethnicities are left outside of these symbolic cultural boundaries. The whiteness of Great Britain's representation in elite cycling international competition is in stark contrast to the multi-ethnic representation that we see today in the Great Britain athletics team, and with the England men's football and cricket teams. 50 years ago, these would have been teams entirely filled with white British athletes. Multi-ethnic representation in the British national cycling team has not transformed with the times. Whiteness dominates.

What seems forgotten is that London won the 2012 Games on an argument and promise that appealed to advancing sport and leisure opportunities with London's unique racial and ethnic diversity; with its everyday lived multiculturalism at heart.

The cycling boom is good. It has created enthusiasm. It created broader appeal for the sport. But this has also given rise to greater divide of opportunity and to segregation in terms of 'race'.

CHAPTER 12 THE NEW TRIBES IN CYCLING

Following the 2012 London Olympics and
the country's cycling boom, more and more
British people are riding bicycles than ever,
and new tribes in cycling have emerged.
I see the MAMIL (Middle Aged Man in
Lycra) finding their sense of youth again
to overcome the onset of a midlife crisis.
I see the newcomer white British middle
class parents and their children equipped
with state-of-the-art campervans and
£10,000 racing bikes at national youth
races. Herd commonality and social
bonding is forged through these new
and exclusive memberships of cultural
existence. But with exclusivity comes
marginalisation. I see some new black
British cycling enthusiasts who claim
to have been made to speak to their
blackness through being marginalised
by these new exclusivities within the sport.
This has resulted in some creating their
own cycling groups, naming them after
their racial and ethnic identities.

Reece Watt, the founder of the Black Cyclists Collective in Leeds, said:

For me, it was a kind of call to action. To let black people and people of colour know that there is a club for them. The other clubs in Leeds do not have people that look like us, and that makes it difficult to approach these clubs. Without representation, many might not even think that cycling is for them. I see this as me doing my bit. BCC stands for diversity and unity, not division. However, The Black Cyclists Collective's name is one that simply outlines the need for more diversity in cycling.

Mani Arthur of the Black Cyclists Network, located in London's Regents Park, said:

We created BCN to create a space so cyclists of colour can feel comfortable entering the sport. We are an inclusive group, not exclusive. We are a Black Cyclists Network in name only. One of the reasons why there is a need for a community like this is cycling is a very white-dominated sport and that can be very intimidating when you are a cyclist of colour.

Temi Lateef of the Black Riders Association, also based in London, said:

I wanted to create a group I felt comfortable in. We are definitely not your average cycling group, and we are specific in regard to who can join our group. I did not start this group to be associated with the national cycling body and have not required any assistance in what I am doing. My question would be how I could help them in their efforts regarding diversity in cycling.

There are cycling groups in North America with similar sentiments. Christopher McGarrell of Man Dem Cycling Club, Toronto, Canada, spoke of building his community club as an escape from "racial affairs", adding: "Everyone – regardless of their identity – deserves a safe space to cycle with others."

Damon Clark Turner of the Los Angeles Bike Academy concurs.

In the early 2000s there were hardly any black cyclists competing, especially juniors. The goal was to provide more opportunities to young riders of colour.

Rachel Olzer, co-founder of Pedal 2 the People – a social media account that features black, indigenous and people of colour – said:

There is always the background stress of being acutely aware of my existence and my presence in a white, male-dominated sport. Being a black cyclist means that I am all too aware that this sport was not built with me in mind.

Saba Ahmed, a leader of the London- and Bristol-based Black Muslim Women Bike group, spoke of the desire to be represented in cycling through the sense of connection and belonging provided by faith and gender. I asked her why the group came into existence.

People deserve to see themselves. By the nature of spaces, be it physical or otherwise, there is a sense of who belongs and who does not. Those who are seen to belong fill these spaces without realising how disconcerting it can be for those who seemingly do not belong. But for those who seemingly do not belong, they have to push to fit in, or feel comfortable. For the person who wants to ride, but does not see themselves in the sport, representation can make a world of difference. We did not see any representation online. Seemingly there was no space for us, though we know there must be many like us, so in short, the rationale was to take up space.

The Women of Colour Cycling Group (WCCG), Evolve – The Cycling Network for Muslim Women, Black Girls Do Bike, and the Sikh Cycling Network are just a few of the many other new collectives of non-white cyclists which can be identified by their gender, faith, or ethnicity. These groups are using social media to communicate their identities in cycling more widely.

The reasons given for founding these groups point to territorial boundaries of access drawn by the cycling community according to 'race'. Entry within these racial boundaries by the non-white cyclist has made them feel alienated and unwelcome. This is why they explicitly use their ethnicity to distinguish themselves as offering a place of inclusion for people of similar identity.

In my experiences of the sport, cycling groups and clubs were generally known by their location. It was this that gave them an identity rather than race, faith, or gender. For example: London Clarion, London Dynamo, Velo Club de Londres, Bec Cycling Club, Catford Cycling Club, Brighton Mitre, Brighton Excelsior, Halesowen Cycling Club, East Bradford Cycling Club. This is neither a definitive nor exhaustive list. Is it not possible for racial, religious, gender diversity to exist within these names?

The argument made by some leaders of the new black British-led groups is that the dominance and exclusivity of white-led and white

THOSE WHO ARE SEEN TO BELONG FILL THESE SPACES WITHOUT REALISING HOW DISCONCERTING IT CAN BE FOR THOSE WHO SEEMINGLY DO NOT BELONG

SABA AHMED

WHEN I WAS GETTING INTO CYCLING, COLOUR JUST DID NOT COME INTO IT. I FEEL LIKE A CYCLIST IN MY OWN RIGHT; LIKE ANY OTHER CYCLIST, WHETHER WHITE, BLACK, OR YELLOW, THERE IS NO PROBLEM

KEVIN RÉZA

populated cycling clubs makes cycling a 'white cyclist's network'. Hence the need to create a space for marginalised black cyclists where they can feel a sense of belonging and connection.

There has been support and praise for this argument as an action of self-empowerment and it has been celebrated by some in the media as trailblazing.

But it seems a racial schism between cycling groups is also being endorsed. The experiences some black cyclists have had in aiming to join all white groups appears to make the creation of all-black groups acceptable. With whom people decide to ride their bikes can now be dictated by the accepted discourse of racial exclusivity in cycling.

This acceptance of racial division in cycling means that, in competition, underlying racial meanings may result in victory for one side being seen as a racial defeat for the other. How far have we come? Are we going backwards, or are we going forwards?

In some ways, Kévin Reza expresses my thoughts on this matter exactly, in his quote on the opposite page.

In my early explorations of the sport, I was not placed in a position where I felt the need to seek out a black-led group or cycling team. In fact, I wasn't really looking to join a club or group. I just loved riding my bike. However, at one point I did bring my bike in for servicing at Brixton Cycles, the cooperative led by the Rastafarian black cyclist Lincoln Romain; just to check things out, to see what was going on.

I also rode by to have a look at De Ver Cycles at one point. I'd read something about doing a ride with a black professional cyclist called Maurice Burton. So, I was curious to find out more. I remember seeing a large group of riders when I got there. Black people and white people all together, dressed in yellow and getting ready to go out on a ride. My first instinct was that I didn't like the colour of the kit.

I hung around for a bit anyway, looking in at the shop and waiting to see what would happen. Nobody talked to me, though, and I didn't get to meet Maurice Burton. So I slipped away and rode off home. It didn't matter.

If I had met Maurice back then, he probably would have talked me out my immediate dislike of his team kit. Maybe he would have got me riding with his multi-ethnic and mixed-gender cycling group.

CHAPTER 13 FACING UP TO ANTI-BLACKNESS

I NEVER FELT I LIKE I FITTED IN. I WAS THE ONLY PERSON OF COLOUR AT BRITISH CYCLING TO START WITH. YOU KNOW, YOU JUST LOOK AROUND YOU AND YOU FEEL DIFFERENT. I DIDN'T FEEL LIKE I FITTED IN

SHANAZE READE

Shanaze Reade in a rare UCI World Cup appearance at Manchester Velodrome 2011

The Black Lives Matter human
rights protests across the world in 2020
exposed how systemic racism of whiteness
is deeply embedded in all aspects
of European and Western societies.
The micro-culture of professional cycling
is not exempt. USA Cycling made a public
statement seemingly wanting to face up to
its contribution to anti-blackness in cycling.
"As the leader of the American cycling
community, USA Cycling understands
we have been part of the problem in the
inequality and representation in our sport.
No amount of talk can change the past,
we must use our position to take
action to embrace, lift up and ride with
the black members of our cycling family
to ensure equality, equity, transparency
and dignity. USA Cycling will use its voice
and position as the national governing
body for a sport that continues to grow
in its inclusion and is committed
to driving necessary change."

However, some grassroots cyclists from the non-white community in the USA do not believe these sorts of statements go far enough. Grace Anderson of PGM ONE (People of the Global Majority in the Outdoors, Nature, and Environment) is among them.

The fight against anti-black racism and white supremacy isn't going to be won with a flimsy Black Lives Matter statement. It's going to take deep systemic change and action. It's going to take white folks in leadership stepping aside for black leadership.

USA Cycling has taken action by forming a partnership with the cycling organisation Black Girls do Bike. The governing body said.

The goal of the partnership is centred around establishing more comfortable places for cyclists in the sport and ushering new riders past barriers to entry and into the larger cycling community, especially women and girls of colour.

Since the governing body's initial statement was issued, however, two prominent young professional riders from the USA – Chloe Dygert and Quinn Simmons – have come under intense public scrutiny for comments on social media perceived as mockery of blackness and dismissal of racism in the sport. Both riders were rebuked by their sponsors and professional teams, but still appear eligible to represent their country. Simmons has said that he did not deserve to be suspended, and that it was internet talk which created the racism, not him.

Rachel Olzer, a cross-country racer and co-founder of Pedal 2 to the People – an Instagram account designed to increase representation of black, indigenous and people of colour in cycling – has emphasised the need to go far beyond stamping out poor individual behaviour such as this.

Getting rid of individual instances of racism toward black or other cyclists of colour will not mean that our problem is solved. Structural racism requires structural changes. We need the industry to take a look at their boards of directors or managers; the athletes they sponsor; the content they produce or share: is it representative of the full range of bicycle users that currently exist? Can we imagine a more inclusive cycling community than the one that we've built?

In Britain, we've not even had the benefit of a clear statement from the national body offering solidarity with the Black Lives Matter anti-

racist human rights movement. This came as a particular
disappointment to me as, in the recent past, I had supported the
organisation and their ethos of 'transforming Britain into a great
cycling nation'. I produced educational materials for their staff and
for dissemination amongst their membership. I provided them with
black British histories in cycling for the promotion of anti-racist
education. This work should, I believe, have provided a strong basis
from which to articulate a position of anti-racist solidarity during
the Black Lives Matter protests across the UK. But nothing came
despite having world-class black BMX riders and coaches, and black
Paralympian cyclists as part of their current squad. The silence from
British Cycling was in stark contrast to the actions of other national
bodies – the Football Association, the England and Wales Cricket
Board, and the Rugby Football Union all publicised their solidarity
with the anti-racist Black Lives Matter human rights protests.

In this context, the British sports media suddenly swarmed
on black athletes, seeking to write about racism including those
experiences of British cyclists. This newly focused interest in the
black experience by the white-dominated media seems to have
given permission for black athletes to breakout from the white
prison of silence that had confined them. Among them, British
parasport athlete Kadeena Cox.

Cycling is dominated by white, middle class people. The colour of my skin determines what opportunities I have; the colour of my skin says there's only room for one or two of us to be accepted in a certain job; the colour of my skin has dictated everything I've done in my whole life. The foundation that is currently in Britain and across the world is against us because we still have to endure systemic racism. That foundation needs to be eradicated and education needs to play a massive part.

Shanaze Reade, the BMX and track cyclist, has also spoken out.

I never felt I like I fitted in. I was the only person of colour at British Cycling to start with. You know, you just look around you and you feel different. I didn't have the backgrounds of some of the other people. I didn't feel like I fitted in. I don't think it was to do with the colour of my skin, but just didn't think I quite fitted in to that British Cycling system. I don't feel like there was any direct racism towards me which is a great position to be in because I know not a lot of people who are mixed race or black can say that within sport.

Riders such as Christian Lyte, Tre Whyte, Russell Williams and Maurice Burton have also shared a sense of not fitting in. But exposing the unreasonable deficits imposed upon black riders by a white-dominated system can sometimes be difficult. If a facility or organisation does not have an electric lift, meaning a building is inaccessible to a wheelchair user, the disadvantage is obvious and the need for change easy to identify. Where a darker-skinned person experiences hypervisibility in a white-dominated space, however, there can be indirect racism and micro aggressive behaviours that may be less immediately obvious.

Some organisations prefer to use terms such as 'diversity' to describe their actions to counter race discrimination. Indeed, British Cycling speaks of its desire to "tackle the diversity gap within British cycling, with a particular focus on increasing black and minority ethnic representation in the racing community, volunteer network, recreation programmes and the organisation's own workforce".

Anti-racism is the unspoken term in this statement and as far back as 2009, Dave Brailsford – the then-head of the GB Olympic cycling team – had spoken of this aim.

Breaking down the barriers to wider participation from black and ethnic minority groups remains the great unconquered goal for British Cycling.

Similarly Brian Cookson, who was president of British Cycling from 1997 to 2013, wrote that "bringing non-white people of all ages into cycling was an aspiration for British Cycling". Yet nearly a quarter of a century on, there is little visible progress towards this goal. This shows that those in positions of power with the ability to make change have always known that non-white people are on the outside, peeping into the British Cycling utopia. Brian Cookson himself has since written that.

I believe the one thing that we did not really address was the subject of the 'whiteness' of the sport... I don't think there was overt or institutional racism as such, but I accept that I am looking at this from a white person's perspective. Clearly, if you look at the numbers, people who are not of a white British ethnicity are under-represented in every facet of cycling.

I doubt the language of 'whiteness' and an understanding of this was being used at the time Cookson was heading up British Cycling. It seems that broadening diverse ethnic representation was a verbal aspiration, but it clearly was not a priority aim. Any broadening of ethnic representation and inclusion in cycling can be stagnated by conservatism and racial prejudice. If the sport is to transform and advance through ethnic diversity, then the priority must be anti-racist education, action and messaging. Here too, though, there is much further to go.

CHAPTER 14 NO MORE NOVELTIES

IN REFERRING TO THEIR WORLD CYCLING CENTRE, THE UCI SAID 2,200 CYCLISTS FROM AROUND THE WORLD HAD PASSED THROUGH THE SYSTEM, YET ONLY GAVE THE NAMES OF TWO BLACK RIDERS: TENIEL CAMPBELL AND DANIEL TEKLEHAIMANOT

Teniel Campbell leads at the Grand Prix De Plouay, France 2019

As the 2020 Tour de France approached,
I prepared for the full range of excitement,
exploits and experiences that cycling's
showcase race always offers. But there
was one sight I knew I wouldn't see.
I absolutely could not imagine any rider
taking the knee or raising a fist in solidarity
with the Black Lives Matter anti-racist
human rights movement. In large part,
that's down to the republican ideal of the
country in which the event takes place.
Issues on 'race' are not allowed to exist.
Recognising the Black Lives Matter
anti-racist human rights movement was
never going to be on the agenda of the
Tour de France organisation. On the
final stage in Paris, some riders did band
together to write anti-racist messages
on their COVID-19 face masks. It was not
an all-in demonstration. But at least some
riders took a lead and were acknowledging
the mood of the people worldwide.

French cyclist Yohann Gène wins at the Tour of Langkawi in Kuala Lumpur in 2009

When the pandemic-interrupted racing season of 2020 restarted with the Strade Bianche on 1st August just a few weeks after the Black Lives Matter protests there was no acknowledgment of the worldwide anti-racist human voice. The UCI issued a statement emphasising "respect of diversity" and that the "federation is closely associated with the symbol of the rainbow – representing the five continents". In referring to their World Cycling Centre in Aigle, Switzerland, they said 2,200 cyclists from around the world had passed through the system, yet only gave the names of two black riders: Teniel Campbell and Daniel Teklehaimanot.

And while its satellite World Cycling Centre in Africa has been credited with supporting many of that continent's most promising riders, some express concern that its good work is being undone. In 2015, Rob Child – a black British sports nutritionist – was working with MTN-Qhubeka, Africa's first ever UCI pro continental team. The squad had notable success at the Tour de France that year, with Teklehaimanot holding the King of the Mountains jersey for several days. Yet Child expressed concern that the roots of such success were already being undermined through a reduction in budget.

So, just as a decade's work by the WCCA come to fruition, the very roots of African cycling's success are under threat. Not only will this impede the UCI's vision to globalise the sport, it will widen the 'performance gap' between African and European racing.

This perspective cautions the apparent progress on anti-racism and representation of black cyclists at WorldTour level which has come via investment in African-based projects, led by the likes of Douglas Ryder, and by the work of Jean-René Bernaudeau to bring talented riders from the French island of Guadeloupe to ride in Europe. This has brought to the world's attention the talents of the likes of Yohan Gène, Merhawi Kudus, and Nicholas Dlamini. So what about Britain? When might it finally have a black rider at the Tour de France? For <u>Mark McKay</u>, several steps will need to take place first.

From my experiences of high-level bike racing, there is no reason that black riders cannot compete well in the Tour de France. However, the journey to the Tour de France starts with filling the pool with enough riders and perhaps requires a specific project over a number of years.

<u>David Clarke</u> emphasises the need for proper support.

For a black British cyclist to compete in the Tour de France? I think could happen. We got to that level [without the help of a team like Team Sky] and we had to fight the system all the way. How good would we have been if we had the backing of British Cycling and WorldTour teams helping us?

Systemic racism embedded in the European cycling framework on which the Tour is built is the significant barrier, says journalist <u>Jeremy Whittle</u>.

There is no willingness to accept the extent of the exclusion of black athletes either at domestic or international level or to instigate genuine change. European cycling still thinks it doesn't have a problem with ethnic diversity, despite everything that has happened in 2020. Given the total absence of black British riders in the WorldTour peloton, and the difficulty in seeing when that will change, it's hard to see a black British rider in the Tour de France in the immediate future.

ITV's Tour de France commentator and cycling writer <u>Ned Boulting</u> expresses a similar opinion.

If Britain were to produce a black Tour rider, then it won't be any time soon. There are, seemingly, no candidates in the pipeline. The number of black riders in the two highest tiers of the sport has been stagnant at best, and in the case of NTT, Africa's only WorldTour team, has actually reduced year-on-year. The British Cycling scene has done nothing to buck that trend.

When I approached Ned's colleague <u>Matt Rendell</u>, I said I thought Britain could produce a black Tour de France winner – after all, man did walk on the moon. He remarked that it was funny I'd phrased it that way.

Nicholas Dlamini leads the peloton over
Boothferry Bridge during stage one of
the Tour de Yorkshire 2019

I had an argument with my editor about Nairo Quintana. I said the journey from where he comes from to the podium of the Tour de France is further, culturally speaking, than the journey it took to put an American on the moon. He told me I was being silly...

To 'walk on the moon' and be the first black British cyclist to race at a Grand Tour will need massive change. But to be 'the first' is not the black man's celebration. The term 'the first' would belong to the gaze of the white world by which 'the first' is framed. And whoever that person is will face a peculiar existence – being 'the first' is an oxymoron; it flits between being a novelty, being revered and being othered. Maurice Burton's experiences speak to this.

In certain cases, the fact that my skin colour was different could have actually been a help. The [track race] promoter wouldn't necessarily want you to beat the local guy. They wouldn't say I was from England; they would say that I was from Jamaica. You know, it sounds more exciting. Because what they want is people to come to the event and they want people to hold that interest like: 'Let's see who this guy is.'

It still happens today. In 2019, in the pouring rain, Nicholas Dlamini led the peloton over Boothferry Bridge during stage one of the Tour de Yorkshire. The photograph of this went viral. It became centre spread of the official programme for the 2019 UCI World Road Race Championships in Harrogate, Yorkshire. It is an incredible photo by Alex Broadway, ultimately shortlisted for a Sports Photography Award. But is part of the reason it gained so much attention the sheer novelty of seeing a black racing cyclist among a sea of white faces? Is it the curiosity of the white gaze that made it so famous?

Sometimes it is clear that black cyclists are being presented to the international stage simply to make up the numbers against more advantaged white competitors. Mark McKay says this was certainly the case at the 2014 and 2018 Commonwealth Games.

I witnessed first-hand how the black nations struggled so much to be able to participate in the racing. It was obvious that most of these nation's bike riders were just making up numbers with inadequate preparation on inadequate kit against the WorldTour level of Australia, New Zealand, Canada and home nations [the UK], not to mention, the rest of the smaller 'white' nations. The black riders were often dropped within the first five to 10 miles of racing on the road and, in track and MTB, within just a few minutes of the start of competition.

Why bother showing up then? This is a demoralising sight for any black person. It is not enough, then, to simply provide opportunities for black cyclists to compete. They need to have access to the same resources that their white counterparts benefit from. This can only advance the sport and make it better. Only through equality of opportunity can we ensure black faces in the peloton and on the track are a normality rather than novelty; are something other than curiosities constructed under a white gaze.

CHAPTER 15 CHANGING THE STORY

RUSSELL WAS MY ROLE MODEL AS A YOUNG BOY. A GREAT MAN WITH A GREAT HEART. FOR ME TO BE HALF THE MAN HE WAS WHEN I GREW UP WOULD HAVE BEEN ENOUGH
BRADLEY WIGGINS

In 2018, I conceived a series of public exhibitions called Made in Britain – Uncovering the Life Histories of Black-British Champions in Cycling. These exhibitions functioned as an educational and anti-racist message; a counterpoint to the misplaced patriotism that morphed into celebratory ethnic nationalism following the country's cycling successes. I included large colourful portraits for each black British cyclist to assist with representing them as icons. I collected photography, memorabilia, medals, jerseys, and trophies from the cyclists. And, viewed together, it had the effect of opening the eyes of many visitors to the names and experiences of the top black British cyclists. This exhibition changed many people's perception of contemporary bike racing culture. Where previously people had only ever seen white faces, they were discovering new names that they had never heard of before.

Bradley Wiggins began to follow the development of my first
exhibition on Instagram. In seeing this, I invited him to conduct
a conversation with Russell Williams for my second exhibition
at Herne Hill Velodrome in June 2019. It turned into an inspirational
reunion for a lot of people who were there, but particularly when
the champion mentee – a white British cycling hero – openly praised
and gave public recognition to one of his early career mentors,
a black British cycling champion.

He was my role model as a young boy.
A great man with a great heart.

For me to be half the man he was when
I grew up would have been enough.

For many visitors, the exhibitions made clear that there has been
a general pattern of unequal treatment of black people in competitive
cycling over the years, and that their representation in the sport
has been close to non-existent compared to white people in all
western countries. I was curious to understand what the cyclists
I'd interviewed for this book thought about the importance of
greater representation. Germain Burton spoke about the need for
black athletes to serve as role models at the elite level of the sport.

If young black people see somebody
in cycling – like they would in football
or boxing – and see them as happy
or successful in what they do, they'll
think: 'Yeah! I'd like to do that as well.'
So, in that respect, it sets people up
with an ambition to be like that as well.
Representation plays a large part of
there not being very many black
British cyclists racing at elite level.
There are not any examples to follow.
For me it was quite straightforward,
I had my dad to follow on from.
Having known that he had been there
and done it I thought, if he did it,
then I could as well.

Russell Williams echoes the need for greater representation.
He adds a point about the increasingly high costs of the sport,
which pose a further discriminatory barrier.

England has fantastic facilities and lots
of cycling tracks if kids want to do it.
There is Manchester, Lee Valley, Derby,
Herne Hill. Yet young black cyclists are
just not coming through. When you don't
see somebody that you recognise, and
winning the races, it doesn't push you
towards it. Cycling is a very expensive
sport. You have to pay to get a licence
to race. You know, if somebody is living
on a council estate trying to survive,
to go out and buy a £2,000 bike is
probably not a priority. It's hard,
very, very hard.

Astana pro and Eritrean national road cycling champion, Merhawi Kudus at the Tour of Switzerland 2019

The financial implications of participating on a level footing is also a point raised by Tim Erwin.

To get more minorities into the sport, I think you have to address the economic hurdle. Cycling is an expensive sport and we all know that in cycling you get what you pay for. A $7,000 bike is better than a $2,000 bike. I'm not saying that you need that calibre of bike to start but the financial issue has to be remedied in order to get increased participation. And when a black rider does show promise they need to be given the same opportunities to train and race and be supported just like anyone else.

Maurice Burton speaks more frankly to these considerations. He suggests the financial output of cycling may be less appealing than opportunities presented in other sports.

Let's step outside of this country for a moment and let's go to Jamaica and let's look at the West Indies cricket team. The team is not as good as it was, say, 30 years ago. Jamaica is a commonwealth country and cricket was a number one sport. Since those days, they have become more involved with the USA and there are now two other avenues in sport: one of them is basketball and the other one is athletics with Usain Bolt. You see Usain Bolt or a top basketball player earning the same if not more money than in cricket.

So when you see a young black person

who has athletic ability, that person could be a cyclist, he could be a track and field athlete and maybe if he is tall enough he could become a basketball player. Look at Joel Garner, the West Indian fast bowler. He was a tall guy. Maybe now he wouldn't have gone to cricket – maybe he would want to go to basketball, where he could potentially earn more money in America.

Going back to this country, what kind of money can a top cyclist earn, and how much money is there in Premier League football? As a young black person with athletic ability, what would your thinking be: football or cycling? With cycling, there is the equipment. There are other avenues in sport that young black people can take to make big money and with less effort really. Maybe it might be seen as too hard. As a cyclist, the training and the fitness, the level that you need to be at is very, very high. You've got to train in bad conditions and for hours on end. You will get some like me. I get up, I go out on the bike, and that's it. Not everybody's mind is that way.

Much of what Maurice says relates to the views of Rahsaan Bahati, who talks of how hard the sport can be both physically and mentally – not necessarily as it may be romantically presented.

Cycling is a tough sport and I know it is not for everyone. The fact of the matter is if you wanna be a bike racer you're going to be a bike racer. You don't have to push. No one had to push me to be a bike racer. All my friends who were pushed by their parents to be cyclists all quit. Every one of them. I can't name one of them that is even riding. Because their parents were so hard on them, and they were pushed to the limit. I was lucky my parents just supported me.

The pattern of thinking seems to be that young black people from Great Britain and the USA may be diverted away from road and track cycling because of these sports being expensive to sustain, and unrewarding in comparison to other sports where the financial benefits are greater. Tre Whyte suggests there is a social elitist air about road and track cycling which can detract black people from thinking about that pathway into the sport.

With track and road cycling, I feel like they are the upper-class sort of sport in cycling. Track and road attracts a big audience, and everybody is into it. People go to watch it because of that. It's a bit like them going to watch golf or tennis at Wimbledon or something. Because of that portrayal, a lot of black people may not be into it. I don't think it is just a white person's sport. But, generally it is dominated by white people.

Erica Elle, a financial professional and founder of the Level Up Cycling Movement, became a UCI rider agent after observing what she saw as grassroots deficiencies for young black athletes.

I became an agent to be a bridge between people of colour and professional cycling. After sitting with a few aspiring young racers and longtime fans of bike racing, it became apparent opportunities for people of colour to race within the US were slim, and at the Continental and WorldTour level basically non-existent.

The lack of access to information was a recurring issue. No one could explain: 'how to become a professional cyclist.'

I watched young people train and race with their hearts first, idolising and studying cycling sensations like Peter Sagan, Mark Cavendish, and Annemiek van Vleuten while in the pit of their guts possessing an understanding that a chance to race as a professional most likely will never arrive. Opportunities for development, high level coaching, support with equipment, and nurturing currently doesn't exist.

Rahsaan Bahati has raised concerns about cycling brands potentially adopting gestural superficial approaches in the name of closing this gap and advancing diversity and inclusion. He speaks to a need for national and world cycling governance to prove and demonstrate a sustainable and lasting commitment to equality.

I mean, there's brands that use black people in their ads and try to use diversity in their campaigns. For me, that's always been a checked box. Like: 'There are more black people buying bikes than ever, we better put them in the ads.' Giant supports me

and my foundation, but that's just a start. That needs to go on continuously for decades. I think they [the bike brands] are starting to turn the corner. Then USA Cycling then the UCI. It won't happen with just the bike brands, though. Everyone has to be on board.

USA Cycling (USAC) has appointed a range of ethnically diverse American athletes, cyclists and activists to its board of directors and sub-committees, including former basketball player Reggie Miller; Lucia Deng, who was formerly a women's representative and licence upgrade coordinator for the New York State Bicycle Racing Association; and Ed Ewing, the co-founder and director of the Major Taylor Project – a youth development cycling initiative focused on creating access and opportunities for people of colour, specifically for youth in diverse and underserved communities.

Power and decision making for the future of cycling in the USA now appears to be being spread amongst ethnically diverse people.

Magazine cover stars past and present:
Wayne Llewellyn *BMX Racer* and *Freestyle* August 1985
Ayesha McGowan *Outside Magazine*/Joao Canziani May 2018
Justin Williams *The Red Bulletin*/Joe Pugliese April 2021
Maurice Burton *Cycling Weekly* April 1974

Another move made by USAC to show a commitment to transforming inclusion in cycling has been to partner with Black Girls Do Bike. Monica Garrison, the founder of this organisation, said.

I think it is important to acknowledge that people of colour can excel at any sport. They don't lack ability. So when you look at the professional and even amateur levels of any sport and you see few faces of colour then you have to ask yourself what is lacking. Is it resources or opportunity or something else?

It looks like the USAC are taking proactive steps to transform the thought processes in the development of cycling. What about Great Britain?

Great Britain has not been able to produce a black road racing or track cycling athlete to represent them at the Olympic Games. At the elite world track championships there have only been Russell Williams and Shanaze Reade. At the elite world road race championships Mark McKay has been the sole representative. I asked some of the cyclists in this book whether black representation could increase in the future and how this could happen. Russell Williams said.

You look at France. They produce fantastic amateur riders. You look at the Netherlands – Ceylin del Carmen Alvarado is now a world champion at cyclo-cross. The African countries are producing riders that are now racing in the Grand Tours. Why is this not happening in Great Britain? We've got the funding. But it really seems to be a black and white issue. Britain can do it. We have got the talent out there.

Maurice Burton also believes in the potential.

I think it can be done. The people in British Cycling must encourage people of colour more. They need to be given hope. It is a lot of work to be able to do these sorts of things. To put that work in, and it doesn't get anywhere, can be very demoralising. The grassroots level of cycling needs to become more accessible. When kids are young at school, they should be encouraged to get into cycling. British Cycling needs to do things higher up, so that any young black rider that comes into their system can feel welcome, supported, and not alienated.

But who is going to protect these young black riders?

Dominant spaces of whiteness must be willing to accept the challenge of education on race consciousness. Some spaces are not ready to commit to this. They fail to realise the benefits of engaging

with broader knowledge and a wider talent pool. The Great Britain athletics team has modelled these benefits over the years. Its current head coach is a black man, the former world champion sprinter Christian Malcolm. Transforming and becoming an ethnically diverse organisation must be genuinely wanted. An overhaul of the entire culture of cycling needs to be undertaken.

Following my engagements with British Cycling before and in the aftermath of the Black Lives Matter anti-racism protests of 2020, the national body established internal and external diversity and inclusion steering groups. Still, unlike USAC, all members of the British Cycling executive board remain white people. Without the challenge of non-white peers as executive board members, there is a risk that a business-as-usual lack of priority thinking on race, ethnicity and inclusion will continue.

One or two elite black road and track riders representing Great Britain at senior level may appear over the next few years and I hope they will be viewed as a sign of successful organisational and cultural change. But at the same time a few non-white faces could be also be open to criticism as being tokenistic; a fast-track surface-level response to the real issues.

Eritrea's Daniel Teklehaimanot
at the prologue of the Tour de France
in Utrecht, The Netherlands 2015

Natnael Berhane in the breakaway as the race passes over the Muur van Geraardsbergen, one of cycling's hallowed hills, stage 1 Tour de France 2019

One view is that there needs to be greater coverage of black cycling athletes being victorious, being happy, as role models for young black people to recognise and to possibly emulate. In the USA, the Williams brothers are framing their sporting identities in this way, as Justin explains.

It's like being in a rock band. You're going to these cities on this tour, and there might be 10,000 people surrounding a crit course, and you're the star of that show.

The Williams brothers wear their national and state championship jerseys with pride. They wear gold chains. They are seen with fast and expensive cars and they have multiple sponsorship deals with international companies. This approach is designed to create and sustain a new dynamic appeal to cycling, as Justin adds.

There's this massive new demographic of people who are looking at the sport, because here are these two black men standing on top of the podium and pushing for change. Whatever people pull from our story – whether it's 'I like the way they dress, so that's why I follow them' or 'These dudes are winning races, so I rock with them' – people are connecting to us.

Perhaps the clearest possibility for seeds of change and a clearer sense of representation at the highest level in cycling is the cycling revolution occurring through the people of Africa. There are some exceptional cycling athletes emerging from Eritrea, such as Natnael Tesfatsion. He follows on from Natnael Berhane and Daniel Teklehaimanot in capturing the imagination of cycling fans. The Ethiopian rider Tsgabu Grmay has also demonstrated his world class talents amongst the best of the Europeans on the world scene.

The African continent is the genuine fertile ground for growing black cycling leaders, role models, and champions who will emerge in greater numbers in the future. The pulse of this movement is being felt. The Tour du Rwanda is now the biggest race in the continent, attracting UCI WorldTour Teams to participate. The UCI World Road Race Championships are set to take place on the African continent in 2025.

Over the years Kenyan and Ethiopian athletes have already risen to dominate endurance track and field athletics at world and Olympic level. All of Ethiopia's Olympic medals have been in long-distance running events. With long term high level financial investment and expertise provided to African cycling, a similar pattern of world-leading excellence could emerge.

The vision of a powerful African team led by black cycling athletes dominating the proceedings in the mountains of the Tour de France, the Giro d'Italia and the Vuelta a España may perhaps be just too great an imaginative concept for the normative cyclical Eurocentric culture of cycling to accept. Too much of an infiltration of black people in its sacred racing spaces, its monuments, its Grand Tours, its history. However, these are just some of the spaces where the genuine revolution can occur to show that cycling is for all. This is a concept that could change the story of cycling and provide opportunity for exciting new chapters in the sport to be written.

References

Introduction
Moncrieffe, M. L. (2016) *Made in Britain: Uncovering the life histories of Black-British champions in cycling* University of Sussex, UK, 14 June

Muhammad Ali Center (2020) 'Red Bike Moment' *alicenter.org*

Chapter 1
Breaking the chain
Biel, J. (2019) 'How Kittie Knox changed bicycling forever' Joe Biel *Medium*, 18 March

Day, R. (1961) 'The Parc gates were shut – but not the road to Rome' *Coureur Sporting Cyclist*, January

Finizon, L. (2020) 'The Outer Line: The Kittie Knox Award – for equity, diversity and inclusion in cycling' *Velonews*, 29 July

Kerber, C. and Kerber, T. (2014) *Major Taylor. The inspiring story of a black cyclist and the men who helped him achieve worldwide fame* New York: Skyhorse Publishing

Miller, G. (2020) *Breaking the Cycle: the Kittie Knox story* Unbound Smithsonian Libraries and Archives, 26 May

Waters, G. (2020) 'Racing in the shadows of mines: Black African cycle sport in South Africa's gold mines during the apartheid era' *classiclightweights.co.uk*, 17 August

Chapter 2
How did you get into it?
Cochrane, A. (2020) 'This Los Angeles Team Wants to Diversify Cycling. They're Starting with Its Podiums' *New York Times*, 1 December

David, M. (2020) 'Why is cycling so white?' *Cycling Weekly*, 2 July

Dowdney, H. (2019) 'This is Justin Williams' *Rapha*, 21 June

Global Cycling Network (2020) 'Making the Coolest Team in Pro Cycling: L39ION Of LA & Justin Williams' *Global Cycling Network (GCN)*, 15 February

Kelly, R. (2019) 'Rahsaan Bahati on Growing up as a Bike Racer in Los Angeles and Making Positive Impacts on Others' *wideanglepodium.com*, 24 September

Weislo, L. (2020) 'Everyday racism: Breaking cycling's other glass ceiling' *Cyclingnews*, 12 June

Woodland, L. (2008) 'Firing for French Gold: Grégory Baugé' *Cyclingnews*, 13 August

Level Up Cycling Movement Inc. (2020) *Being Black in Cycling*, 8 June

Chapter 3
What the fucking hell are you doing here with us?
Coulon, J. (2020) 'Here's What You Need to Know About French Pro Cyclist Kévin Reza' *Bicycling.com*, 11 September

Delaney, B. (2020) 'A conversation on racism in cycling with Dr. Tim Erwin' *Velonews*, 10 June

Dlamini, N. (2020) 'Capricorn Star' *The Road Book* London: Olympia Publishers

Keith, P. (2020) 'Being Black in Cycling' *Level Up Cycling Movement*, 8 June

Kerber, C. and Kerber, T. (2014) *Major Taylor. The inspiring story of a black cyclist and the men who helped him achieve worldwide fame* New York: Skyhorse Publishing

Weislo, L. (2020) 'Everyday racism: Breaking cycling's other glass ceiling' *Cyclingnews*, 12 June

Woodland, L. (2008) 'Firing for French Gold: Grégory Baugé' *Cyclingnews*, 13 August

Chapter 4
Let your legs to do the talking!
Woodland, L. (2008) 'Firing for French Gold: Grégory Baugé' *Cyclingnews*, 13 August

Chapter 7
The Dark Destroyer
Delaney, B. (2020) 'A conversation on racism in cycling with Dr. Tim Erwin' *Velonews*, 10 June

timetriallingforum.co.uk (2009) *Whites only?*, 3 June

Chapter 9
It wasn't going to happen
Weislo, L. (2020) 'Everyday racism: Breaking cycling's other glass ceiling' *Cyclingnews*, 12 June

Chapter 10
Adventure and Survival
Cochrane, A. (2020) 'This Los Angeles Team Wants to Diversify Cycling. They're Starting with Its Podiums' *New York Times*, 1 December

Delves, J. (2020) 'The invisible champion' *Cyclist*, issue 104, September

Global Cycling Network (2020) 'Making the Coolest Team in Pro Cycling: L39ION Of LA & Justin Williams' *Global Cycling Network (GCN)*, 15 February

Long, J. (2020) 'Justin Williams' Legion of Los Angeles raise $50k for cycling diversity fund' *Cycling Weekly*, 8 June

Long, J. (2019) 'US road champion Justin Williams: "Being in a sport that is primarily white it was hard not to feel alone, it broke me"' *Cycling Weekly*, 3 June.

Weislo, L. (2020) 'Everyday racism: Breaking cycling's other glass ceiling' *Cyclingnews*, 12 June

Chapter 11
The Velodrome of Whiteness
British Cycling (2016) 'British Cycling reaches 125,000 members' *British Cycling*, 16 August

Wynn, N. (2015) 'Why right now is Britain's golden age of cycling' *Cycling Weekly*, 4 August

British Cycling (2019) 'British Cycling reaches 150,000 members' *British Cycling*

Chapter 12
New tribes in cycling
Clarke, R. (2020) 'Black Cyclists Network: Founder Mani Arthur on creating pathway for BAME riders' *Sky Sports Cycling News*, 29 September

Coulon, J. (2020) 'Here's What You Need to Know About French Pro Cyclist Kévin Reza' *Bicycling.com*, 11 September

Olzer, R. (2020) 'What it Means to Never See Black People Out Riding' *Bicycling*, 27 July

Chapter 13
Facing up to Anti-Blackness
Anderson, G. (2020) 'Claiming Our Sport Is Color Blind Isn't Helping Black People' *Bicycling*, 27 July

Barbet, M. (2020) 'Shanaze Reade on Lancashire Lockdown' *Home Roads*, 28 October

Bloom, B. (2020) 'Kadeena Cox interview: "A cyclist said racism does not exist in Britain. Are you serious?"' *The Daily Telegraph*, 25 June

British Cycling (2020) 'British Cycling Launches Project to Tackle Diversity Gap in Cycling' *British Cycling*, 29 October

Cookson, B. (2020) 'British Cycling on my watch' *briancookson.com/british-cycling*

Moncrieffe, M. L. (2016) *Made in Britain: Uncovering the life histories of Black-British champions in cycling* University of Sussex, UK, 14 June

Long, J. (2021) 'Quinn Simmons says he did not deserve to be suspended over black hand emoji incident' *Cycling Weekly*, 27 February

Olzer, R. (2020) 'What it Means to Never See Black People Out Riding' *Bicycling*, 27 July

Pool, B. (2020) 'USA Cycling and Black Girls Do Bike announce partnership to make cycling more accessible to women of colour' *usacycling.org*, 13 August

Seaton, M. (2009) 'Why is cycling such a "white" sport?' *The Guardian*, 10 August

Chapter 14
No more novelties
Child, R. (2015) 'African cycling: as the world celebrates recent successes are its very roots under threat' *Velowire.com*, 13 August

Moncrieffe, M. L. (2021) 'How do we applaud anti-racist action in cycling beyond a sense of tokenistic superficiality?' *Advancing Anti-Racism in Cycling*, 19 February

Moncrieffe, M. (2020) 'Tour de France 2020: professional cycling's history of anti-blackness', London: *The Conversation*, 26 August

Moncrieffe, M. (2020) 'When will Britain have a black rider in the Tour?' *Procycling*, issue 273, October

Union Cycliste Internationale (2020) 'The UCI for diversity in cycling' *uci.org*, 9 June

Weislo, L. (2020) 'Everyday racism: Breaking cycling's other glass ceiling' *Cyclingnews*, 12 June

Chapter 15
Changing the story
Welch, B. (2020) Rahsaan Bahati: 'I've had to conform to get my foot in the door' *Velonews*, 4 June

Elle, F. (2020) 'When I Started Riding, I Was Treated Like I Didn't Exist' *Bicycling*, 27 July

Delaney, B. (2020) 'A conversation on racism in cycling with Dr. Tim Erwin' *Velonews*, 10 June

Garrison, M. (2020) 'If You Love Cycling, You Need to Have Uncomfortable Conversations About Race' *Bicycling*, 27 July

Kelly, R. (2019) 'Rahsaan Bahati on Growing up as a Bike Racer in Los Angeles and Making Positive Impacts on Others' *wideanglepodium.com*, 24 September

Liu, G. (2021) 'Justin Williams Wants You to Care About Pro Cycling' *Outside*, 12 April

Moncrieffe, M. (2018) *Centring the career narratives of Black-British champion cyclists within the context of nation, nationalism and identity* British Society of Sports History Annual Conference, 20 September

Moncrieffe, M. (2019) *Made in Britain: Uncovering the life histories of Black-British Champions in British Cycling: An Exhibition concerning Excellence, Representation and Diversity* British Cycling Hub, UCI World Championships, Harrogate, Yorkshire, 21, 22 September

Moncrieffe, M. (2019) *"From Grassroots to Glory" Made in Britain: Uncovering the life histories of Black-British champions in cycling* The Big Velo Fete, Herne Hill Velodrome, London. 15, 16 June

Moncrieffe, M. (2018) *Made in Britain: Uncovering the life-histories of Black-British Champions in Cycling*. University of Brighton, Grand Parade Galleries, Brighton, 10-20 December.

Made in Britain Exhibition

The Made in Britain exhibitions changed many people's perception of contemporary bike racing culture. Where previously people had only ever seen white faces, they were discovering new names that they had never heard before. Visitors were also struck by these cyclists' desire and determination in overcoming implicit and explicit racial discrimination in cycling. Just a few of the comments from members of the public who viewed the exhibitions held in Brighton, 2018 and at the Herne Hill Velodrome 2019:

"I discovered new names that I had never heard of before I was here"

"I didn't realise how many black riders there were"

"Fascinating exhibition telling an important story!"

"The personal stories have been excellent. Really illuminating. I think the combination of photos, objects and testimonies works really well. I now have a heightened awareness of black achievement in cycling."

"I didn't realise that there were so many brilliant black cyclists"

"I have been able to gain knowledge that I didn't know"

"I wasn't aware of the under-representation of the black cyclists' contribution to the sport"

"Fascinating, heartwarming histories that demonstrate determination, grit and staying power"

"Every one of them experienced discrimination. It's a massive shame on the sport"

"This exhibition highlights a side to cycling I had never seen before. The determination to get to where they had; then for it to be taken away makes you question society"

"Their dedication to their chosen sport. Their love of it despite the barriers they faced."

"I feel angry for the lost opportunities for some of these great riders"

Typefaces

Body type in this book is set in Dapifer, by Darden Studio. Darden Studio was founded by African American typeface designer Joshua Darden and is continued by Joyce Ketterer. *dardenstudio.com*
Headlines and pull quotes throughout the book are set in Martin by Vocal Type. Martin is a non-violent display typeface inspired by those used on civil rights signs and 1960s demonstration posters. Vocal Type was founded by Tré Seals and aims to introduce a diverse perspective to the typographic world. *vocaltype.co*

Editor's Thanks

Many thanks to Marlon, and to all those riders he collaborated with, in realising this ground-breaking book. Thanks also to Simon Mottram, Tom McMullen, Ger Tierney, Matt Tucker, Francois Convercey and Melissa Richards at Rapha and Rapha Editions for being so supportive of the project and having the foresight to publish it. Many thanks to designer Leo Field and to Linda Duong and Keith George who made all the pictures print 'just so'. To our tireless copy editor Claire Read, whose patient suggestions and corrections are always very welcome: many thanks, Claire.

One of the most challenging parts of realising this book was the invisibility of black riders in cycling photography – just finding images of those riders Marlon speaks about, past and present. That photographic invisibility certainly amplifies the absence they have had in the media.

You'll notice from the long list of picture credits that many of the photographs for this book have come from a variety of sources beyond the usual archives. Riders' friends, family and the riders themselves helped us, digging into their personal collections, and we're hugely grateful for everyone's efforts to get their images to us. Special thanks to those who gave us permission to use images too, notably Vern Pitt from *Cycling Weekly* and Paul Jones for the last minute scans, to John Bradley and Jon Dorn from *Outside* magazine and to Rudi Uebelhoer and Ruth McLeod from *The Red Bulletin*. Thanks also to Jeremy Dunn and Herbie Sykes for all their efforts and support.

And lastly a big shout-out to those who enthusiastically helped us track down photos by digging around in cupboards, attics and garages, notably Dale Holmes, Scott Dick, Rashid Bahati, Barbara George, Mark Noble, Gerrit Does, Bart de Jong and an extra special thank you to Dom Phipps. We are immensely grateful to you all.

Guy Andrews

Author's Thanks

A chequered flag is the symbol of victory, completion and emancipation: black and white combined. The cycling universe conspired and connected me on this ride. The privilege of me writing this book could not have been realised without the generosity from the cyclists I have learned from along the course, particularly: Maurice Burton, Russell Williams, David Clarke, Charlie Reynolds, Christian Lyte, Charlotte Cole-Hossain, Tre Whyte, Quillan Isidore, Germain Burton, Justin Williams, Rahsaan Bahati, Marie-Divine Kouamé Taky, Grégory Baugé, Kévin Reza, Nelson Vails, Wayne Llewellyn and Luli Adeyamo.

In production of this book, huge thanks to the Bluetrain publishing team led by Guy Andrews and Taz Darling. Credit to Guy for his outstanding support during the redrafting processes. Credit to Taz for her excellent selection and arrangement of photography and illustrations. Lastly, a massive thanks to the Rapha Editions team led by Simon Mottram and Tom McMullen.

Marlon Lee Moncrieffe

WE GOT TO THAT
LEVEL WITHOUT ANY
HELP AND WE
HAD TO FIGHT THE
SYSTEM ALL THE WAY.
HOW GOOD WOULD
WE HAVE BEEN IF
WE HAD THE BACKING
OF BRITISH CYCLING
AND WORLDTOUR
TEAMS HELPING US?
DAVID CLARKE